Washington
Rules of Evidence
Handbook

with
Common Objections
&
Evidentiary Foundations

2023

(Last amended Jan. 2023)

Professor John Barkai
&
Kira J. Goo

William S. Richardson School of Law
University of Hawaii

Cover colors are from the Washington state flag

What's upfront? Traditionally, the first few pages of a book include information about formatting, copyright, dedication, and other such topics before getting to the substance of the text. However, because the unique and most valuable sections in this handbook (Objections & Foundations) follow the rules section, and because Amazon's "Look inside" feature does not show samples sections of later pages which might make this handbook most attractive to you, I will place some sample pages of the Objections and Foundations material upfront directly after the content/index pages.

Regarding copyright – there is none. Of course, there is no claim to copyright the Washington Rules of Evidence, "a work prepared by an officer or employee of the United States Government as part of that person's official duties." In addition, I give you permission to freely copy and use other sections of this handbook, including the sections on objections and evidentiary foundations, under a Creative Commons Attribution (CCBY) 4.0 License, which essentially means that you may use, share, or adapt the information in these pages for any purpose, even commercial, if you give "appropriate credit" and indicate changes you made, if any. Please cite the material as: John Barkai & Kira J. Goo, Washington Rules of Evidence Handbook with Common Objections & Evidentiary Foundations. Also, you cannot restrict others from using these materials.

Formatting. There seems to be no standard formatting style for presenting the rules of evidence. This handbook uses formatting intended to make the understanding and application of the rules as clear as possible - but clarity and ease of understanding of the rules of evidence by using the text alone is almost impossible. Font may vary, using larger fonts for rules you are likely to consult more often and smaller fonts for rules less likely to be consulted.

Disclaimer: The authors and publisher are offering no legal advice. Your trial judge may view the law and foundations differently. The law is whatever the judge in your case says it is. Any errors in this book are mine.

Corrections, omissions, suggestions?
See any or have some? Contact me at barkai@hawaii.edu

Recent Amendment: R1101(c)(4) effective Jan. 1, 2023 ("chapters 7.105 and 74.34 RCW" and "they do not")

Common Citation Forms: ER xxx or even WRE xxx.

Washington Rules of Evidence Handbook
with
Common Objections
&
Evidentiary Foundations

Professor John Barkai
William S. Richardson School of Law
University of Hawaii
Honolulu, HI 96822
Jan. 2023

ISBN: 9798725652345

INTRODUCTION

**This Washington Rules of Evidence Handbook
was designed to be brought to court and be at your side in the office.**

Besides the rules of evidence, the **"added value"** in this handbook is the following useful and entertaining sections:

A) **Making and Responding to Common Objections** (16 pages)
  - a discussion of the most common objections
  - a list of the most common objections
B) **Evidentiary Foundations and Impeachment** (over 60 pages)
  - 25 examples of the most common evidentiary foundations
  - a brief discussion of differing standards for authenticating digital evidence (such as email, text messages, social media sites, and internet sites)

The sample foundation and impeachment questions are "bare-bones" foundations which include the minimum questions and answers necessary to get testimony or exhibits admitted into evidence

Professor John Barkai

SUMMARY OF CONTENTS

Appendix

Expanded Appendix
Making and Responding to Common Objections A-1

Evidentiary Foundations...A-17

Make an Objection in Four Steps

1) Stand up.
2) Say, "Objection ____" (Fill in the blank with your reason).
3) Identify your specific objection.
    a) At a minimum, say the topic type
       (Hearsay, Relevance, Improper Impeachment, Improper
       Character, Lack of Foundation, Leading Question, etc.)
    b) State the evidence rule number if you know it (404, 608, etc.).
    c) A combination of the above
       ("Objection, Improper Impeachment, R613")
4) Stop talking and listen to the judge.
    Be prepared to state reasons for your objection and to make an
    argument to support your position.

How to Respond to An Objection?

1) Speak to the judge, not the lawyer who objected.
2) Explain to the judge why your evidence should be admissible.
    ("Your Honor, that statement is not hearsay because I am not
    offering it for the truth but rather to show notice.")
3) If you recognize that you did not lay an appropriate foundation
for the evidence explain that you will do that. ("Your Honor, I will
lay the foundation.")
4) If you recognize that the opposing counsel was objecting to the
form of your question, which most often happens on your direct
examination, simply say, "I'll rephrase." Rephrase the question and
move on with your witness examination. Do not get sidetracked by
the opposing counsel who might have objected just to throw you off
track.
5) For any physical piece of evidence, statement, or testimony that
you will be introducing, prepare in advance and have a reason why
you believe that evidence is admissible. Be ready to make that
argument to the judge.
6) If the objection is to relevance, and you think you will be able to
show that it is relevant, say to the judge "I will connect it up in a few
questions Your Honor." Such a statement is equivalent of saying
"trust me." If you do that, you'd better connect it up or the judge
will not trust you in the future.

A List of Common Possible Objections

Ambiguous	Improper opinion
Argumentative	Improper rehabilitation
Asked and answered	Inadmissible opinion
Assumes facts not in evidence	Incompetent witness
Authentication	Incomplete Inflammatory
Badgering	Insufficient foundation
Best evidence	Irrelevant (Relevance)
Beyond the scope	Lack of foundation
Bias	Lack of personal knowledge
Bolstering	Leading question
Calls for a conclusion	Misleading
Calls for speculation	Misquotes a witness or exhibit
Chain of custody	Misquotes evidence
Collateral	Misstates witness
Competence	More prejudicial than probative
Compound question	Motion to strike
Compromise / Settlement offer	Narrative
Confrontation (lack of)	(Question calls for a narrative)
Confusing	Narrative answer
Counsel is testifying	Non-responsive
Cumulative	Nothing pending
Document speaks for itself	Outside the scope of cross
Expert (Improper opinion)	Overly broad or general
Expert (not qualified)	Parole evidence rule
Habit	Personal knowledge
Harassing the witness	Prejudice (unfair)
Hearsay	Privilege communication
Hypothetical question misused	Relevance
Improper character evidence	Speculation/ Opinion/ Lack of
Improper characterization	personal knowledge
Improper impeachment	Unintelligible
	Vague

There are many more possible objections,
limited only by the lawyer's imagination.

Judges and the local legal culture in your jurisdiction may have other rules or approaches to objections that are not touched on in this handbook. Ask around and learn about them.

Authentication of Text Message – An Example

Text Message

Received by Witness

Do you know Y?

Do you communicate with Y on a regular basis?

In what ways to you communicate with Y?

Did you receive a text message from the Y [recently; on or about _ date, on the topic of …, etc.]?

Would you recognize a printout of the message if you were to see it again?

Let me show you what has been marked as proposed exhibit # 1. Do you recognize it?

What is it? [Ans: A screenshot from my cell phone]

How do you know that this is a message from Y? [It is similar to other messages I have received from Y in that …]

How did it appear when it arrived on your phone? [Showed up under the name and with the picture I had previously assigned to Y]

What other distinctive characteristics did you notice about the message? [provide as many as distinctive characteristics possible]

Is it a fair and accurate representation of the text message you received [recently; on or about _ date, on the topic of visiting your son, etc.]?

Has it been altered in any way?

I would like to enter the proposed exhibit into evidence

WASHINGTON RULES OF EVIDENCE
(Last amended Jan. 2023)

TITLE 1 GENERAL PROVISIONS

TITLE 2 JUDICIAL NOTICE

TITLE 3 PRESUMPTIONS IN CIVIL ACTIONS AND PROCEEDINGS

TITLE 4 RELEVANCY AND ITS LIMITS

TITLE 5 PRIVILEGES

TITLE 6 WITNESSES

The Most Commonly Used
Washington Hearsay Sub-Sections

WASHINGTON RULES OF EVIDENCE

TITLE I. GENERAL PROVISIONS

Rule 101. Scope

These rules govern proceedings in the courts of the state of Washington to the extent and with the exceptions stated in rule 1101.

Rule 102. Purpose and Construction

These rules shall be construed to secure fairness in administration, elimination of unjustifiable expense and delay, and promotion of growth and development of the law of evidence to the end that the truth may be ascertained and proceedings justly determined.

Rule 103. Rulings on Evidence

(a) Effect of Erroneous Ruling. Error may not be predicated upon a ruling which admits or excludes evidence unless a substantial right of the party is affected, and

(1) Objection. In case the ruling is one admitting evidence, a timely objection or motion to strike is made, stating the specific ground of objection, if the specific ground was not apparent from the context; or

(2) Offer of Proof. In case the ruling is one excluding evidence, the substance of the evidence was made known to the court by offer or was apparent from the context within which questions were asked.

(b) Record of Offer and Ruling. The court may add any other or further statement which shows the character of the evidence, the form in which it was offered, the objection made, and the ruling thereon. The court may direct the making of an offer in question and answer form.

(c) Hearing of Jury. In jury cases, proceedings shall be conducted, to the extent practicable, so as to prevent inadmissible evidence from being suggested to the jury by any means, such as making statements or offers of proof or asking questions in the hearing of the jury.

(d) Errors Raised for the First Time on Review. [Reserved - See RAP 2.5(a).]

Rule 104. Preliminary Questions

(a) Questions of Admissibility Generally. Preliminary questions concerning the qualification of a person to be a witness, the existence of a privilege, or the admissibility of evidence shall be determined by the court, subject to the provisions of section (b). In making its determination it is not bound by the Rules of Evidence except those with respect to privileges.

(b) Relevancy Conditioned on Fact. When the relevancy of evidence depends upon the fulfillment of a condition of fact, the court shall admit it upon, or subject to, the introduction of evidence sufficient to support a finding of the fulfillment of the condition.

(c) Hearing of Jury. Hearings on the admissibility of confessions shall in all cases be conducted out of the hearing of the jury. Hearings on other preliminary matters shall be so conducted when the interests of justice require or, when an accused is a witness and so requests.

(d) Testimony by Accused. The accused does not, by testifying upon a preliminary matter, become subject to cross examination as to other issues in the case.

(e) Weight and Credibility. This rule does not limit the right of a party to introduce before the jury evidence relevant to weight or credibility.

Rule 105. Limited Admissibility

When evidence which is admissible as to one party or for one purpose but not admissible as to another party or for another purpose is admitted, the court, upon request, shall restrict the evidence to its proper scope and instruct the jury accordingly.

Rule 106. Remainder of or Related Writings or Recorded Statements

When a writing or recorded statement or part thereof is introduced by a party, an adverse party may require the party at that time to introduce any other part, or any other writing or recorded statement, which ought in fairness to be considered contemporaneously with it.

TITLE II. JUDICIAL NOTICE

Rule 201. Judicial Notice of Adjudicative Facts

(a) Scope of Rule. This rule governs only judicial notice of adjudicative facts.

(b) Kinds of Facts. A judicially noticed fact must be one not subject to reasonable dispute in that it is either (1) generally known within the territorial jurisdiction of the trial court or (2) capable of accurate and ready determination by resort to sources whose accuracy cannot reasonably be questioned.

(c) When Discretionary. A court may take judicial notice, whether requested or not.

(d) When Mandatory. A court shall take judicial notice if requested by a party and supplied with the necessary information.

(e) Opportunity to Be Heard. A party is entitled upon timely request to an opportunity to be heard as to the propriety of taking judicial notice and the tenor of the matter noticed. In the absence of prior notification, the request may be made after judicial notice has been taken.

(f) Time of Taking Notice. Judicial notice may be taken <u>at any stage</u> of the proceeding.

TITLE III. PRESUMPTIONS IN CIVIL ACTIONS AND PROCEEDINGS

Rule 301. Presumptions in General in Civil Actions and Proceedings
(Reserved)

Rule 302. Applicability of State Law in Civil Actions and Proceedings
(Reserved)

TITLE IV. RELEVANCE AND ITS LIMITS

Rule 401. Definition of "Relevant Evidence"
"Relevant evidence" means evidence having any tendency to make the existence of any fact that is of consequence to the determination of the action more probable or less probable than it would be without the evidence.

Rule 402. Relevant Evidence Generally Admissible; Irrelevant evidence Inadmissible
All relevant evidence is admissible, except as limited by constitutional requirements or as otherwise provided by statute, by these rules, or by other rules or regulations applicable in the courts of this state. Evidence which is not relevant is not admissible.

Rule 403. Exclusion of Relevant Evidence on Grounds of Prejudice, Confusion, or Waste of Time
Although relevant, evidence may be excluded if its probative value is substantially outweighed by the danger of unfair prejudice, confusion of the issues, or misleading the jury, or by considerations of undue delay, waste of time, or needless presentation of cumulative evidence.

Rule 404. Character Evidence Not Admissible to Prove Conduct; Exceptions; Other Crimes
(a) Character Evidence Generally. Evidence of a person's character or a trait of character is not admissible for the purpose of proving action in conformity therewith on a particular occasion, except:

(1) Character of Accused. Evidence of a pertinent trait of character offered by an accused, or by the prosecution to rebut the same;

(2) Character of Victim. Evidence of a pertinent trait of character of the victim of the crime offered by an accused, or by the prosecution to rebut the same, or evidence of a character trait of peacefulness of the victim offered by the prosecution in a homicide case to rebut evidence that the victim was the first aggressor;

(3) Character of Witness. Evidence of the character of a witness, as provided in rules 607, 608, and 609.

(b) Other Crimes, Wrongs, or Acts. Evidence of other crimes, wrongs, or acts is not admissible to prove the character of a person in order to show action in conformity therewith. It may, however, be admissible for other purposes, such as proof of motive, opportunity, intent, preparation, plan, knowledge, identity, or absence of mistake or accident.

4

Rule 405. Methods of Proving Character

(a) Reputation. In all cases in which evidence of character or a trait of character of a person is admissible, proof may be made by testimony as to reputation. On cross examination, inquiry is allowable into relevant specific instances of conduct.

(b) Specific Instances of Conduct. In cases in which character or a trait of character of a person is an essential element of a charge, claim, or defense, proof may also be made of specific instances of that person's conduct.

Rule 406. Habit; Routine Practice

Evidence of the habit of a person or of the routine practice of an organization, whether corroborated or not and regardless of the presence of eyewitnesses, is relevant to prove that the conduct of the person or organization on a particular occasion was in conformity with the habit or routine practice.

Rule 407. Subsequent Remedial Measures

When, after an event, measures are taken which, if taken previously, would have made the event less likely to occur, evidence of the subsequent measures is not admissible to prove negligence or culpable conduct in connection with the event. This rule does not require the exclusion of evidence of subsequent measures when offered for another purpose, such as proving ownership, control, or feasibility of precautionary measures, if controverted, or impeachment.

Rule 408. Compromise and Offers to Compromise

In a civil case, evidence of (1) furnishing or offering or promising to furnish, or (2) accepting or offering or promising to accept a valuable consideration in compromising or attempting to compromise a claim which was disputed as to either validity or amount, is not admissible to prove liability for or invalidity of the claim or its amount. Evidence of conduct or statements made in compromise negotiations is likewise not admissible. This rule does not require exclusion of any evidence otherwise discoverable merely because it is presented in the course of compromise negotiations. This rule also does not require exclusion when the evidence is offered for another purpose, such as proving bias or prejudice of a witness, negating a contention of undue delay, or proving an effort to obstruct a criminal investigation or prosecution.

Rule 413. Immigration Status

(a) Criminal Cases; Evidence Generally Inadmissible. In any criminal matter, evidence of a party's or a witness's immigration status shall not be admissible unless immigration status is an essential fact to prove an element of, or a defense to, the criminal offense with which the defendant is charged, or to show bias or prejudice of a witness pursuant to ER 607. The following procedure shall apply prior to any such proposed uses of immigration status evidence to show bias or prejudice of a witness:

(1) A written pretrial motion shall be made that includes an offer of proof of the relevancy of the proposed evidence.

(2) The written motion shall be accompanied by an affidavit or affidavits in which the offer of proof shall be stated.

(3) If the court finds that the offer of proof is sufficient, the court shall order a hearing outside the presence of the jury.

(4) The court may admit evidence of immigration status to show bias or prejudice if it finds that the evidence is reliable and relevant, and that its probative value outweighs the prejudicial nature of evidence of immigration status.

(5) Nothing in this section shall be construed to exclude evidence that would result in the violation of a defendant's constitutional rights.

(b) Civil Cases; Evidence Generally Inadmissible. Except as provided in subsection (b)(1), evidence of a party's or a witness's immigration status shall not be admissible unless immigration status is an essential fact to prove an element of a party's cause of action.

(1) Posttrial Proceedings. Evidence of immigration status may be submitted to the court through a posttrial motion:

(A) where a party, who is subject to a final order of removal in immigration proceedings, was awarded damages for future lost earnings; or

(B) where a party was awarded reinstatement to employment.

(2) Procedure to Review Evidence. Whenever a party seeks to use or introduce immigration status evidence, the court shall conduct an in camera review of such evidence. The motion, related papers, and record of such review may be sealed pursuant to GR 15, and shall remain under seal unless the court orders otherwise. If the court determines that the evidence may be used, the court shall make findings of fact and conclusions of law regarding the permitted use of that evidence.

TITLE V. PRIVILEGES

Rule 501. General Rule

The following citations are to certain statutes that make reference to privileges or privileged communications. This list is not intended to create any privilege, nor to abrogate any privilege by implication or omission.

(a) Attorney-Client. (Reserved. See RCW 5.60.060(2).)

(b) Clergyman or Priest. (Reserved. See RCW 5.60.060(3), 26.44.060, 70.124.060.)

(c) Dispute Resolution Center. (Reserved. See RCW 7.75.050.)

(d) Counselor. (Reserved. See RCW 18.19.180.)

(e) Higher Education Procedures. (Reserved. See RCW 28B.19.120(4).)

(f) Spouse or Domestic Partner. (Reserved. See RCW 5.60.060(1), 26.20.071, 26.21A275(8).)

(g) Interpreter in Legal Proceeding. (Reserved. See RCW 2.42.160; GR 11.1(e).)

(h) Journalist. (Reserved. See RCW 5.68.010.)

(i) Optometrist-Patient. (Reserved. See RCW 18.53.200, 26.44.060.)

(j) Physician-Patient. (Reserved. See RCW 5.60.060(4), 26.26.120, 26.44.060, 51.04.050, 69.41.020, 69.50.403, 70.124.060, 71.05.250.)

(k) Psychologist-Client. (Reserved. See RCW 18.83.110, 26.44.060, 70.124.060.)

(l) Public Assistance Recipient. (Reserved. See RCW 74.04.060.)

(m) Public Officer. (Reserved. See RCW 5.60.060(5).)

(n) Registered Nurse. (Reserved. See RCW 5.62.010, 5.62.020, 5.62.030

Rule 502. Attorney-Client Privilege and Work Product; Limitations on Waiver

The following provisions apply, in the circumstances set out, to disclosure of a communication or information covered by the attorney-client privilege or work-product protection.

(a) Disclosure Made in a Washington Proceeding or to a Washington Office or Agency; Scope of a Waiver. When the disclosure is made in a Washington proceeding or to a Washington office or agency and waives the attorney-client privilege or work-product protection, the waiver extends to an undisclosed communication or information in any proceeding only if:

(1) the waiver is intentional;

(2) the disclosed and undisclosed communications or information concern the same subject matter; and

(3) they ought in fairness be considered together.

(b) Inadvertent Disclosure. When made in a Washington proceeding or to a Washington office or agency, the disclosure does not operate as a waiver in any proceeding if:

(1) the disclosure is inadvertent;

(2) the holder of the privilege or protection took reasonable steps to prevent disclosure; and

(3) the holder promptly took reasonable steps to rectify the error, including (if applicable) following 26(b)(6).

(c) Disclosure Made in a Non-Washington Proceeding. When the disclosure is made in a non-Washington proceeding and is not the subject of a court order concerning waiver, the disclosure does not operate as a waiver in a Washington proceeding if the disclosure:

(1) would not be a waiver under this rule if it had been made in a Washington proceeding; or

(2) is not a waiver under the law of the jurisdiction where the disclosure occurred.

(d) Controlling Effect of a Court Order. A Washington court may order that the privilege or protection is not waived by disclosure connected with the litigation pending before the court—in which event the disclosure is also not a waiver in any other proceeding.

(e) Controlling Effect of a Party Agreement. An agreement on the effect of disclosure in a Washington proceeding is binding only on the parties to the agreement, unless it is incorporated into a court order.

(f) Definitions. In this rule:

(1) "attorney-client privilege" means the protection that applicable law provides for confidential attorney-client communications; and

(2) "work-product protection" means the protection that applicable law provides for tangible material (or its intangible equivalent) prepared in anticipation of litigation or for trial.

TITLE VI. WITNESSES

Rule 601. General Rule of Competency
Every person is competent to be a witness except as otherwise provided by statute or by court rule

Rule 602. Lack of Personal Knowledge
A witness may not testify to a matter unless evidence is introduced sufficient to support a finding that the witness has personal knowledge of the matter. Evidence to prove personal knowledge may, but need not, consist of the witness' own testimony. This rule is subject to the provisions of rule 703, relating to opinion testimony by expert witnesses.

Rule 603. Oath or Affirmation
Before testifying, every witness shall be required to declare that the witness will testify truthfully, by oath or affirmation administered in a form calculated to awaken the witness' conscience and impress the witness' mind with the duty to do so.

Rule 604. Interpreters
An interpreter is subject to the provisions of these rules relating to qualification as an expert and the administration of an oath or affirmation to make a true translation.

Rule 605. Competency of Judge as Witness
The judge presiding at the trial may not testify in that trial as a witness. No objection need be made in order to preserve the point.

Rule 606. Competency of Juror as Witness
A member of the jury may not testify as a witness before that jury in the trial of the case in which the juror is sitting. If the juror is called so to testify, the opposing party shall be afforded an opportunity to object out of the presence of the jury.

Rule 607. Who May Impeach
The credibility of a witness may be attacked by any party, including the party calling the witness.

Rule 608. Evidence of Character and Conduct of Witness
(a) Reputation Evidence of Character. The credibility of a witness may be attacked or supported by evidence in the form of reputation, but subject to the limitations:

(1) the evidence may <u>refer only to character for truthfulness or untruthfulness</u>, and

(2) evidence of truthful character is admissible only after the character of the witness for truthfulness has been <u>attacked by reputation evidence or otherwise</u>.

(b) Specific Instances of Conduct. Specific instances of the conduct of a witness, for the purpose of attacking or supporting the witness' credibility, other than conviction of crime as provided in rule 609, may <u>not</u> be proved by <u>extrinsic evidence</u>. They may, however, in the <u>discretion</u> of the court, if probative of truthfulness or untruthfulness, be inquired into on <u>cross</u> examination of the witness

(1) concerning the <u>witness' character</u> for truthfulness or untruthfulness, or

(2) concerning the <u>character</u> for truthfulness or untruthfulness <u>of another witness</u> as to which character the witness being cross-examined has testified.

Rule 609. Impeachment by Evidence of Conviction of Crime
(a) General Rule. For the purpose of attacking the credibility of a witness in a criminal or civil case, evidence that the witness has been convicted of a crime shall be admitted if elicited from the witness or established by public record during examination of the witness but only if the crime (1) was punishable by death or imprisonment in excess of 1 year under the law under which the witness was convicted, and the court determines that the probative value of admitting this evidence outweighs the prejudice to the party against whom the evidence is offered, or (2) involved dishonesty or false statement, regardless of the punishment.
(b) Time Limit. Evidence of a conviction under this rule is not admissible if a period of more than 10 years has elapsed since the date of the conviction or of the release of the witness from the confinement imposed for that conviction, whichever is the later date, unless the court determines, in the interests of justice, that the probative value of the conviction supported by specific facts and circumstances substantially outweighs its prejudicial effect. However, evidence of a conviction more than 10 years old as calculated herein, is not admissible unless the proponent gives to the adverse party sufficient advance written notice of intent to use such evidence to provide the adverse party with a fair opportunity to contest the use of such evidence.
(c) Effect of Pardon, Annulment, or Certificate of Rehabilitation. Evidence of a conviction is not admissible under this rule if (1) the conviction has been the subject of a pardon, annulment, certificate of rehabilitation, or other equivalent procedure based on a finding of the rehabilitation of the person convicted, and that person has not been convicted of a subsequent crime which was punishable by death or imprisonment in excess of 1 year, or (2) the conviction has been the subject of a pardon, annulment, or other equivalent procedure based on a finding of innocence.
(d) Juvenile Adjudications. Evidence of juvenile adjudications is generally not admissible under this rule. The court may, however, in a criminal case allow evidence of a finding of guilt in a juvenile offense proceeding of a witness other than the accused if conviction of the offense would be admissible to attack the credibility of an adult and the court is satisfied that admission in evidence is necessary for a fair determination of the issue of guilt or innocence.
(e) Pendency of Appeal. The pendency of an appeal therefrom does not render evidence of a conviction inadmissible. Evidence of the pendency of an appeal is admissible.

Rule 610. Religious Beliefs or Opinions
Evidence of the beliefs or opinions of a witness on matters of religion is not admissible for the purpose of showing that by reason of their nature the witness' credibility is impaired or enhanced.

Rule 611. Mode and Order of Interrogation and Presentation
(a) Control by Court. The court shall exercise reasonable control over the mode and order of interrogating witnesses and presenting evidence so as to
(1) make the interrogation and presentation effective for the ascertainment of the truth,
(2) avoid needless consumption of time, and
(3) protect witnesses from harassment or undue embarrassment.
(b) Scope of Cross Examination. Cross examination should be limited to the subject matter of the direct examination and matters affecting the credibility of the witness. The court may, in the exercise of discretion, permit inquiry into additional matters as if on direct examination.
(c) Leading Questions. Leading questions should not be used on the direct examination of a witness except as may be necessary to develop the witness' testimony. Ordinarily leading questions should be permitted on cross examination. When a party calls a hostile witness, an adverse party, or a witness identified with an adverse party, interrogation may be by leading questions.

Rule 612. Writing Used to Refresh Memory
If a witness uses a writing to refresh memory for the purpose of testifying, either:
while testifying, or
before testifying, if the court in its discretion determines it is necessary in the interests of justice,
an adverse party is entitled
to have the writing produced at the hearing,
to inspect it,
to cross-examine the witness thereon, and
to introduce in evidence those portions which relate to the testimony of the witness.
If it is claimed that the writing contains matters not related to the subject matter of the testimony, the court shall examine the writing in camera, excise any portions not so related, and order delivery of the remainder to the party entitled thereto. Any portion withheld over objections shall be preserved and made available to the appellate court in the event of an appeal. If a writing is not produced or delivered pursuant to order under this rule, the court shall make any order justice requires.

Rule 613. Prior Statements of Witnesses

(a) Examining Witness Concerning Prior Statement. In the examination of a witness concerning a prior statement made by the witness, whether written or not, the court may require that the statement be shown or its contents disclosed to the witness at that time, and on request the same shall be shown or disclosed to opposing counsel.

(b) Extrinsic Evidence of Prior Inconsistent Statement of Witness. Extrinsic evidence of a prior inconsistent statement by a witness is not admissible <u>unless</u> the witness is afforded <u>an opportunity to explain or deny</u> the same and the opposite party is afforded an opportunity to interrogate the witness thereon, or the interests of justice otherwise require. This provision does not apply to admissions of a party-opponent as defined in rule 801(d)(2).

Rule 614. Calling and Interrogation of Witnesses by Court

(a) Calling by Court. The court may, on its own motion where necessary in the interests of justice or on motion of a party, call witnesses, and all parties are entitled to cross-examine witnesses thus called.

(b) Interrogation by Court. The court may interrogate witnesses, whether called by itself or by a party; provided, however, that in trials before a jury, the court's questioning must be cautiously guarded so as not to constitute a comment on the evidence.

(c) Objections. Objections to the calling of witnesses by the court or to interrogation by it may be made at the time or at the next available opportunity when the jury is not present.

Rule 615. Exclusion of Witnesses

At the request of a party the court may order witnesses excluded so that they cannot hear the testimony of other witnesses, and it may make the order of its own motion. This rule does not authorize exclusion of

(1) a party who is a natural person, or

(2) an officer or employee of a party which is not a natural person designated as its representative by its attorney, or

(3) a person whose presence is shown by a party to be reasonably necessary to the presentation of the party's cause.

TITLE VIII. HEARSAY

Rule 801. Definitions

The following definitions apply under this article:

(a) Statement. A "statement" is (1) an oral or written assertion or (2) nonverbal conduct of a person, if it is intended by the person as an assertion.

(b) Declarant. A "declarant" is a person who makes a statement.

(c) Hearsay. "Hearsay" is a statement, other than one made by the declarant while testifying at the trial or hearing, offered in evidence to prove the truth of the matter asserted.

(d) Statements Which Are Not Hearsay. A statement is not hearsay if--

    (1) Prior Statement by Witness. The declarant testifies at the trial or hearing and is subject to cross examination concerning the statement, and the statement is

        (i) inconsistent with the declarant's testimony, and was given under oath subject to the penalty of perjury at a trial, hearing, or other proceeding, or in a deposition, or

        (ii) consistent with the declarant's testimony and is offered to rebut an express or implied charge against the declarant of recent fabrication or improper influence or motive, or

        (iii) one of identification of a person made after perceiving the person; or

(2) Admission by Party-Opponent. The statement is offered against a party and is

        (i) the party's own statement, in either an individual or a representative capacity or

        (ii) a statement of which the party has manifested an adoption or belief in its truth, or

        (iii) a statement by a person authorized by the party to make a statement concerning the subject, or

        (iv) a statement by the party's agent or servant acting within the scope of the authority to make the statement for the party, or

        (v) a statement by a coconspirator of a party during the course and in furtherance of the conspiracy.

Rule 802. Hearsay Rule

Hearsay is not admissible except as provided by these rules, by other court rules, or by statute.

Rule 803. Hearsay Exceptions; Availability of Declarant Immaterial
(a) Specific Exceptions. The following are not excluded by the hearsay rule, even though the declarant is available as a witness:

(1) Present Sense Impression. A statement describing or explaining an event or condition made while the declarant was perceiving the event or condition, or immediately thereafter.

(2) Excited Utterance. A statement relating to a startling event or condition made while the declarant was under the stress of excitement caused by the event or condition.

(3) Then Existing Mental, Emotional, or Physical Condition. Statement of the declarant's then existing state of mind, emotion, sensation, or physical condition (such as intent, plan, motive, design, mental feeling, pain, and bodily health), but not including a statement of memory or belief to prove the fact remembered or believed unless it relates to the execution, revocation, identification, or terms of declarant's will.

(4) Statements for Purposes of Medical Diagnosis or Treatment. Statements made for purposes of medical diagnosis or treatment and describing medical history, or past or present symptoms, pain, or sensations, or the inception or general character of the cause or external source thereof insofar as reasonably pertinent to diagnosis or treatment.

(5) Recorded Recollection. A memorandum or record concerning a matter about which a witness once had knowledge but now has insufficient recollection to enable the witness to testify fully and accurately, shown to have been made or adopted by the witness when the matter was fresh in the witness' memory and to reflect that knowledge correctly. If admitted, the memorandum or record may be read into evidence but may not itself be received as an exhibit unless offered by an adverse party.

(6) Records of Regularly Conducted Activity. (Reserved. See RCW 5.45.)

[RCW 5.45.020 Business records as evidence.
A record of an act, condition or event, shall in so far as relevant, be competent evidence if the custodian or other qualified witness testifies to its identity and the mode of its preparation, and if it was made in the regular course of business, at or near the time of the act, condition or event, and if, in the opinion of the court, the sources of information, method and time of preparation were such as to justify its admission.]

(7) Absence of Entry in Records Kept in Accordance with RCW 5.45.
Evidence that a matter is not included in the memoranda, reports, records, or data compilations, in any form, kept in accordance with the provisions of RCW 5.45, to prove the nonoccurrence or nonexistence of the matter, if the matter was of a kind of which a memorandum, report, record, or data compilation was regularly made and preserved, unless the sources of information or other circumstances indicate lack of trustworthiness.

(8) Public Records and Reports. (Reserved. See RCW 5.44.040.)
[**RCW 5.44.040 Certified copies of public records as evidence.**
Copies of all records and documents on record or on file in the offices of the various departments of the United States and of this state or any other state or territory of the United States or any federally recognized Indian tribe, when duly certified by the respective officers having by law the custody thereof, under their respective seals where such officers have official seals, must be admitted in evidence in the courts of this state.]

(9) Records of Vital Statistics. Records or data compilations, in any form, of births, fetal deaths, deaths, or marriages, if the report thereof was made to a public office pursuant to requirements of law.

(10) Absence of Public Record or Entry. To prove the absence of a record, report, statement, or data compilation, in any form, or the nonoccurrence or nonexistence of a matter of which a record, report, statement, or data compilation, in any form, was regularly made and preserved by a public office or agency, evidence in the form of a certification in accordance with rule 902, or testimony, that diligent search failed to disclose the record, report, statement, or data compilation, or entry.

(11) Records of Religious Organizations. Statements of births, marriages, divorces, deaths, legitimacy, ancestry, relationship by blood or marriage, or other similar facts of personal or family history, contained in a regularly kept record of a religious organization.

(12) Marriage, Baptismal, and Similar Certificates. Statements of fact contained in a certificate that the maker performed a marriage or other ceremony or administered a sacrament, made by a clergyman, public official, or other person authorized by the rules or practices of a religious organization or by law to perform the act certified, and purporting to have been issued at the time of the act or within a reasonable time thereafter.

(13) Family Records. Statements of fact concerning personal or family history contained in family Bibles, genealogies, charts, engravings on rings, inscriptions on family portraits, tattoos, engravings on urns, crypts, or tombstones, or the like.

(14) Records of Documents Affecting an Interest in Property. The record of a document purporting to establish or affect an interest in property, as proof of the content of the original recorded document and its execution and delivery by each person by whom it purports to have been executed, if the record is a record of a public office and an applicable statute authorized the recording of documents of that kind in that office.

(15) Statements in Documents Affecting an Interest in Property. A statement contained in a document purporting to establish or affect an interest in property if the matter stated was relevant to the purpose of the document unless dealings with the property since the document was made have been inconsistent with the truth of the statement or the purport of the document.

(16) Statements in Ancient Documents. Statements in a document in existence 20 years or more whose authenticity is established.

(17) Market Reports, Commercial Publications. Market quotations, tabulations, lists, directories, or other published compilations, generally used and relied upon by the public or by persons in particular occupations.

(18) Learned Treatises. To the extent called to the attention of an expert witness upon cross examination or relied upon by the expert witness in direct examination, statements contained in published treatises, periodicals, or pamphlets on a subject of history, medicine, or other science or art, established as a reliable authority by the testimony or admission of the witness or by other expert testimony or by judicial notice. If admitted, the statements may be read into evidence but may not be received as exhibits.

(19) Reputation Concerning Personal or Family History. Reputation among members of a person's family by blood, adoption, or marriage, or among a person's associates, or in the community, concerning a person's birth, adoption, marriage, divorce, death, legitimacy, relationship by blood, adoption, or marriage, ancestry, or other similar fact of a person's personal or family history.

(20) Reputation Concerning Boundaries or General History. Reputation in a community, arising before the controversy, as to boundaries of or customs affecting lands in the community, and reputation as to events of general history important to the community or state or nation in which located.

(21) Reputation as to Character. Reputation of a person's character among his associates or in the community

(22) Judgment of Previous Conviction. Evidence of a final judgment, entered after a trial or upon a plea of guilty (but not upon a plea of nolo contendere), adjudging a person guilty of a crime punishable by death or imprisonment in excess of 1 year, to prove any fact essential to sustain the judgment, but not including, when offered by the prosecution in a criminal case for purposes other than impeachment, judgments against persons other than the accused. The pendency of an appeal may be shown but does not affect admissibility.

(23) Judgment as to Personal, Family, or General History, or Boundaries. Judgments as proof of matters of personal, family, or general history, or boundaries, essential to the judgment, if the same would be provable by evidence of reputation.

(b) Other Exceptions. (Reserved.)

Rule 804. Hearsay Exceptions; Declarant Unavailable

(a) Definition of Unavailability. "Unavailability as a witness" includes situations in which the declarant:

(1) Is exempted by ruling of the court on the ground of <u>privilege</u> from testifying concerning the subject matter of the declarant's statement; or

(2) <u>Persists in refusing</u> to testify concerning the subject matter of the declarant's statement despite an order of the court to do so; or

(3) Testifies to a <u>lack of memory</u> of the subject matter of the declarant's statement; or

(4) Is unable to be present or to testify at the hearing because of <u>death or then existing physical or mental illness or infirmity</u>; or

(5) Is <u>absent</u> from the hearing and the proponent of the statement has been <u>unable to procure the declarant's attendance</u> (or in the case of a hearsay exception under subsection (b)(2), (3), or (4), the declarant's attendance or testimony) by process or other reasonable means.

(6) A declarant is <u>not unavailable</u> as a witness if the exemption, refusal, claim of lack of memory, inability, or absence is due to the procurement or <u>wrongdoing</u> of the proponent of a statement for the purpose of preventing the witness from attending or testifying.

(b) Hearsay Exceptions. The following are not excluded by the hearsay rule if the declarant is unavailable as a witness:

(1) Former Testimony. Testimony given as a witness at another hearing of the same or a different proceeding, or in a deposition taken in compliance with law in the course of the same or another proceeding, if the party against whom the testimony is now offered, or, in a civil action or proceeding, a predecessor in interest, had an opportunity and similar motive to develop the testimony by direct, cross, or redirect examination.

(2) Statement Under Belief of Impending Death. In a trial for homicide or in a civil action or proceeding, a statement made by a declarant while believing that the declarant's death was imminent, concerning the cause or circumstances of what the declarant believed to be the declarant's impending death.

(3) Statement Against Interest. A statement which was at the time of its making so far contrary to the declarant's pecuniary or proprietary interest, or so far tended to subject the declarant to civil or criminal liability, or to render invalid a claim by the declarant against another, that a reasonable person in the declarant's position would not have made the statement unless the person believed it to be true. In a criminal case, a statement tending to expose the declarant to criminal liability is not admissible unless corroborating circumstances clearly indicate the trustworthiness of the statement.

(4) Statement of Personal or Family History.

(i) A statement concerning the declarant's own birth, adoption, marriage, divorce, legitimacy, relationship by blood, adoption, or marriage, ancestry, or other similar fact of personal or family history, even though declarant had no means of acquiring personal knowledge of the matter stated; or

(ii) a statement concerning the foregoing matters, and death also, of another person, if the declarant was related to the other by blood, adoption, or marriage or was so intimately associated with the others family as to be likely to have accurate information concerning the matter declared.

(5) Other Exceptions. (Reserved.)

(6) Forfeiture by Wrongdoing. A statement offered against a party that has engaged directly or indirectly in wrongdoing that was intended to, and did, procure the unavailability of the declarant as a witness.

Rule 805. Hearsay Within Hearsay

Hearsay included within hearsay is not excluded under the hearsay rule if each part of the combined statements conforms with an exception to the hearsay rule provided in these rules.

Rule 806. Attacking and Supporting Credibility of Declarant
When a hearsay statement, or a statement defined in rule 801(d)(2)(iii), (iv), or (v), has been admitted in evidence, the credibility of the declarant may be attacked, and if attacked may be supported, by any evidence which would be admissible for those purposes if declarant had testified as a witness. Evidence of a statement or conduct by the declarant at any time, inconsistent with the declarant's hearsay statement, is not subject to any requirement that the declarant may have been afforded an opportunity to deny or explain. If the party against whom a hearsay statement has been admitted calls the declarant as a witness, the party is entitled to examine the declarant on the statement as if under cross examination.

Rule 807. Child Victims or Witnesses
(Reserved. See RCW 9A.44.120.)

TITLE IX. AUTHENTICATING OR IDENTIFYING EVIDENCE

Rule 901. Requirement of Authentication or Identification

(a) General Provision. The requirement of authentication or identification as a condition precedent to admissibility is satisfied by evidence sufficient to support a finding that the matter in question is what its proponent claims.

(b) Illustrations. By way of illustration only, and not by way of limitation, the following are examples of authentication or identification conforming with the requirements of this rule:

(1) Testimony of Witness with Knowledge. Testimony that a matter is what it is claimed to be.

(2) Nonexpert Opinion on Handwriting. Nonexpert opinion as to the genuineness of handwriting, based upon familiarity not acquired for purposes of the litigation.

(3) Comparison by Court or Expert Witness. Comparison by the court or by expert witnesses with specimens which have been authenticated.

(4) Distinctive Characteristics and the Like. Appearance, contents, substance, internal patterns, or other distinctive characteristics, taken in conjunction with circumstances.

(5) Voice Identification. Identification of a voice, whether heard firsthand or through mechanical or electronic transmission or recording, by opinion based upon hearing the voice at any time under circumstances connecting it with the alleged speaker.

(6) Telephone Conversations. Telephone conversations, by evidence that a call was made to the number assigned at the time by the telephone company to a particular person or business, if (i) in the case of a person, circumstances, including self-identification, show the person answering to be the one called, or (ii) in the case of a business, the call was made to a place of business and the conversation related to business reasonably transacted over the telephone.

(7) Public Records or Reports. (Reserved. See RCW 5.44 and CR 44.)

(8) Ancient Documents or Data Compilation. Evidence that a document or data compilation, in any form, (i) is in such condition as to create no suspicion concerning its authenticity, (ii) was in a place where it, if authentic, would likely be, and (iii) has been in existence 20 years or more at the time it is offered.

(9) Process or System. Evidence describing a process or system used to produce a result and showing that the process or system produces an accurate result.

(10) Electronic Mail (E-mail). Testimony by a person with knowledge that (i) the e-mail purports to be authored or created by the particular sender or the sender's agent; (ii) the e-mail purports to be sent from an e-mail address associated with the particular sender or the sender's agent; and (iii) the appearance, contents, substance, internal patterns, or other distinctive characteristics of the e-mail, taken in conjunction with the circumstances, are sufficient to support a finding that the e-mail in question is what the proponent claims.

(11) Methods Provided by Statute or Rule. Any method of authentication or identification provided by statute or court rule.

Rule 902. Self-Authentication

Extrinsic evidence of authenticity as a condition precedent to admissibility is not required with respect to the following:

(a) Domestic Public Documents Under Seal. A document bearing a seal purporting to be that of the United States, or of any state, district, commonwealth, territory, or insular possession thereof, or the Panama Canal Zone, or the Trust Territory of the Pacific Islands, or of a political subdivision, department, officer, or agency thereof, and a signature purporting to be an attestation or execution.

(b) Domestic Public Documents Not Under Seal. A document purporting to bear the signature in the official capacity of an officer or employee of any entity included in section (a), having no seal, if a public officer having a seal and having official duties in the district or political subdivision of the officer or employee certifies under seal that the signer has the official capacity and that the signature is genuine.

(c) Foreign Public Documents. A document purporting to be executed or attested in an official capacity by a person authorized by the laws of a foreign country to make the execution or attestation, and accompanied by a final certification as to the genuineness of the signature and official position (1) of the executing or attesting person, or (2) of any foreign official whose certificate of genuineness of signature and official position relates to the execution or attestation or is in a chain of certificates of genuineness of signature and official position relating to the execution or attestation. A final certification may be made by a secretary of embassy or legation, consul general, consul, vice-consul, or consular agent of the United States, or a diplomatic or consular official of the foreign country assigned or accredited to the United States. If reasonable opportunity has been given to all parties to investigate the authenticity and accuracy of official documents, the court may, for good cause shown, order that they be treated as presumptively authentic without final certification or permit as presumptively authentic without final certification or permit them to be evidenced by an attested summary with or without final certification.

(d) Certified Copies of Public Records. A copy of an official record or report or entry therein, or of a document authorized by law to be recorded or filed and actually recorded or filed in a public office, including data compilations in any form, certified as correct by the custodian or other person authorized to make the certification, by certificate complying with section (a), (b), or (c) of this rule or complying with any applicable law, treaty or convention of the United States, or the applicable law of a state or territory of the United States.

(e) Official Publications. Books, pamphlets, or other publications purporting to be issued by public authority.

(f) Newspapers and Periodicals. Printed materials purporting to be newspapers or periodicals.

(g) Trade Inscriptions and the Like. Inscriptions, signs, tags, or labels purporting to have been affixed in the course of business and indicating ownership, control, or origin.

(h) Acknowledged Documents. Documents accompanied by a certificate of acknowledgment executed in the manner provided by law by a notary public or other officer authorized by law to take acknowledgments.

(i) Commercial Paper and Related Documents. Commercial paper, signatures thereon, and documents relating thereto to the extent provided by general commercial law.

(j) Presumptions Created by Law. Any signature, document, or other matter declared by any law of the United States or of this state to be presumptively or prima facie genuine or authentic.

Rule 903. Subscribing Witness' Testimony Unnecessary

The testimony of a subscribing witness is not necessary to authenticate a writing unless required by the laws of the jurisdiction whose laws govern the validity of the writing.

Rule 904. Admissibility of Documents

(a) Certain Documents Admissible. In a civil case, any of the following documents proposed as exhibits in accordance with section (b) of this rule shall be deemed admissible unless objection is made under section (c) of this rule:

(1) A bill, report made for the purpose of treatment, chart, record of a hospital, doctor, dentist, registered nurse, licensed practical nurse, physical therapist, psychologist or other health care provider, on a letterhead or billhead;

(2) A bill for drugs, medical appliances or other related expenses on a letterhead or billhead;

(3) A bill for, or an estimate of, property damage on a letterhead or billhead. In the case of an estimate, the party intending to offer the estimate shall forward a copy to the adverse party with a statement indicating whether or not the property was repaired, and if it was, whether the estimated repairs were made in full or in part and attach a copy of the receipted bill showing the items of repair and amounts paid;

(4) A weather or traffic signal report, or standard United States government table;

(5) A photograph, x-ray, drawing, map, blueprint or similar documentary evidence;

(6) A document not specifically covered by any of the foregoing provisions but relating to a material fact and having equivalent circumstantial guaranties of trustworthiness, the admission of which would serve the interests of justice.

(b) Notice. Any party intending to offer a document under this rule must serve on all parties a notice, no less than 30 days before trial, stating that the documents are being offered under Evidence Rule 904 and shall be deemed authentic and admissible without testimony or further identification, unless objection is served within 14 days of the date of notice, pursuant to ER 904(c). The notice shall be accompanied by (1) numbered copies of the documents and (2) an index, which shall be organized by document number and which shall contain a brief description of the document along with the name, address and telephone number of the document's author or maker. The notice shall be filed with the court. Copies of documents that accompany the notice shall not be filed with the court.

(c) Objection to Authenticity or Admissibility. Within 14 days of notice, any other party may serve on all parties a written objection to any document offered under section (b), identifying each document to which objection is made by number and brief description.

(1) If an objection is made to a document on the basis of authentication, and if the court finds that the objection was made without reasonable basis, the offering party shall be entitled to an award of expenses and reasonable attorney fees incurred as a result of the required proof of authentication as to each such document determined to be authentic and offered as an exhibit at the time of trial.

(2) If an objection is made to a document on the basis of admissibility, the grounds for the objection shall be specifically set forth, except objection on the grounds of relevancy need not be made until trial. If the court finds that the objection was made without reasonable basis and the document is admitted as an exhibit at trial, the court may award the offering party any expenses incurred and reasonable attorney fees.

(d) Effect of Rule. This rule does not restrict argument or proof relating to the weight to be accorded the evidence submitted, nor does it restrict the trier of fact's authority to determine the weight of the evidence after hearing all of the evidence and the arguments of opposing parties.

TITLE X. CONTENTS OF WRITINGS, RECORDINGS, AND PHOTOGRAPHS

Rule 1001. Definitions

For purposes of this article the following definitions are applicable:

(a) Writings and Recordings. "Writings" and "recordings" consist of letters, words, sounds, or numbers, or their equivalent, set down by handwriting, typewriting, printing, photostating, photographing, magnetic impulse, mechanical or electronic recording, or other form of data compilation.

(b) Photographs. "Photographs" include still photographs, X-ray films, videotapes, and motion pictures.

(c) Original. An "original" of a writing or recording is the writing or recording itself or any counterpart intended to have the same effect by a person executing or issuing it. An "original" of a photograph includes the negative or any print therefrom. If data are stored in a computer or similar device, any printout or other output readable by sight, shown to reflect the data accurately, is an "original".

(d) Duplicate. A "duplicate" is a counterpart produced by the same impression as the original, or from the same matrix, or by same impression as the original, or from the same matrix, or by means of photography, including enlargements and miniatures, or by mechanical or electronic recording, or by chemical reproduction, or by other equivalent techniques which accurately reproduce the original.

Rule 1002. Requirement of Original

To prove the content of a writing, recording, or photograph, the original writing, recording, or photograph is required, except as otherwise provided in these rules or by rules adopted by the Supreme Court of this state or by statute.

Rule 1003. Admissibility of Duplicates

A duplicate is admissible to the same extent as an original unless (1) a genuine question is raised as to the authenticity of the original or (2) in the circumstances it would be unfair to admit the duplicate in lieu of the original.

Rule 1004. Admissibility of Other Evidence of Contents

The original is not required, and other evidence of the contents of a writing, recording, or photograph is admissible if:

(a) Original Lost or Destroyed. All originals are lost or have been destroyed, unless the proponent lost or destroyed them in bad faith; or

(b) Original Not Obtainable. No original can be obtained by any available judicial process or procedure; or

(c) Original in Possession of Opponent. At a time when an original was under the control of the party against whom offered, that party was put on notice, by the pleadings or otherwise, that the contents would be a subject of proof at the hearing, and that party does not produce the original at the hearing; or

(d) Collateral Matters. The writing, recording, or photograph is not closely related to a controlling issue.

Rule 1005. Public Records

The contents of an official record, or of a document authorized to be recorded or filed and actually recorded or filed, including data compilations in any form, if otherwise admissible, may be proved by copy, certified as correct in accordance with rule 902 or testified to be correct by a witness who has compared it with the original. If a copy which complies with the foregoing cannot be obtained by the exercise of reasonable diligence, then other evidence of the contents may be given.

Rule 1006. Summaries

The contents of voluminous writings, recordings, or photographs which cannot conveniently be examined in court may be presented in the form of a chart, summary, or calculation. The originals, or duplicates, shall be made available for examination or copying, or both, by other parties at reasonable time and place. The court may order that they be produced in court.

Rule 1007. Testimony or Written Admission of Party

Contents of writings, recordings, or photographs may be proved by the testimony or deposition of the party against whom offered or by that party's written admission, without accounting for the nonproduction of the original.

Rule 1008. Functions of Court and Jury

When the admissibility of other evidence of contents of writings, recordings, or photographs under these rules depends upon the fulfillment of a condition of fact, the question whether the condition has been fulfilled is ordinarily for the court to determine in accordance with the provisions of rule 104. However, when an issue is raised (1) whether the asserted writing ever existed, or (2) whether another writing, recording, or photograph produced at the trial is the original, or (3) whether other evidence of contents correctly reflects the contents, the issue is for the trier of fact to determine as in the case of other issues of fact.

TITLE 11 MISCELLANEOUS RULES

Rule 1101. Applicability of Rules

(a) Courts Generally. Except as otherwise provided in section (c), these rules apply to all actions and proceedings in the courts of the state of Washington. The terms "judge" and "court" in these rules refer to any judge of any court to which these rules apply or any other officer who is authorized by law to hold any hearing to which these rules apply.

(b) Law with Respect to Privilege. The law with respect to privileges applies at all stages of all actions, cases, and proceedings.

(c) When Rules Need Not Be Applied. The rules (other than with respect to privileges, the rape shield statute and ER 412) need not be applied in the following situations:

(1) Preliminary Questions of Fact. The determination of questions of fact preliminary to admissibility of evidence when the issue is to be determined by the court under rule 104(a).

(2) Grand Jury. Proceedings before grand juries and special inquiry judges.

(3) Miscellaneous Proceedings. Proceedings for extradition or rendition; detainer proceedings under RCW 9.100; preliminary determinations in criminal cases; sentencing, or granting or revoking probation; issuance of warrants for arrest, criminal summonses, and search warrants; proceedings with respect to release on bail or otherwise; contempt proceedings in which the court may act summarily; habeas corpus proceedings; small claims court; supplemental proceedings under RCW 6.32; coroners' inquests; preliminary determinations in juvenile court; juvenile court hearings on declining jurisdiction; disposition, review, and permanency planning hearings in juvenile court; dispositional determinations related to treatment for alcoholism, intoxication, or drug addiction under RCW 70.96A; and dispositional determinations under RCW 71.05 and 71.34.

(4) Applications for Protection Orders. Protection order proceedings under chapters 7.105 and 74.34 RCW. Provided when a judge proposes to consider information from a criminal or civil database, the judge shall disclose the information to each party present at the hearing; on timely request, provide each party with an opportunity to be heard; and take appropriate measures to alleviate litigants' safety concerns. The judge has discretion not to disclose information that they do not propose to consider.

(d) Arbitration Hearings. In a mandatory arbitration hearing under RCW 7.06, the admissibility of evidence is governed by MAR 5.3.

Rule 1102. Amendments (Reserved)

Rule 1103. Title

These rules may be known and cited as the Washington Rules of Evidence. ER is the official abbreviation.

Making and Responding to Common Objections

Professor John Barkai

> This section provides ideas about making and responding to common objections, and includes a list of common objections.

An almost endless number of objections could be made at trial. Many lists, "cheat sheets," and articles about objections can be found on the internet. This section of the book will summarize those resources, discuss the basics about objections, and provide a list of the more common objections.

Why Do Lawyers Object?
Lawyers object to:

1) limit the information fact finder can consider
   by excluding testimony, witnesses, or exhibits offered by the opposing party,

2) control the opposing lawyer's conduct
   by preventing certain questions or answers, the calling of certain witnesses, and certain statements from being made during opening statements or closing arguments,

3) preserve errors for appeal,

4) disrupt opponent's counsel's momentum,

5) send a signal to a witness,

6) communicate with the fact finder, and

7) give the witness a break and time to think.

Lawyers frequently object to the form of question (Argumentative, Ambiguous, Vague, Asked and Answered, etc.) to prevent the judge or jury from hearing inadmissible evidence. Often, however, such objections are made simply to harass, annoy, upset, or distract opposing counsel. The less experience the lawyer has, the more such objections are likely to distract. Some people consider objections made for such purposes to be "unethical;" other people consider such objections part of the competition in the adversary system. Whatever your view, be ready for such objections.

Make an Objection in Four Steps

1) Stand up.
2) Say, "Objection _____ " (Fill in the blank with your reason).
3) Identify your specific objection.
   a) At a minimum, say the topic type
      (Hearsay, Relevance, Improper Impeachment, Improper
      Character, Lack of Foundation, Leading Question, etc.)
   b) State the evidence rule number if you know it (404, 608, etc.).
   c) A combination of the above
      ("Objection, Improper Impeachment, R613")
4) Stop talking and listen to the judge.
   Be prepared to state reasons for your objection and to make an
   argument to support your position.

How to Respond to an Objection

1) Speak to the judge, not the lawyer who objected.
2) Explain to the judge why your evidence should be admissible.
   ("Your Honor, that statement is not hearsay because I am not
   offering it for the truth, but rather to show notice.")
3) If you recognize that you did not lay an appropriate foundation
   for the evidence, explain that you will do that. ("Your Honor, I
   will lay the foundation.")
4) If you recognize that the opposing counsel was objecting to the
   form of your question, which most often happens on your direct
   examination, simply say, "I'll rephrase." Rephrase the question
   and move on with your witness examination. Do not get
   sidetracked by the opposing counsel who might have objected
   just to throw you off track.
5) For any physical piece of evidence, statement, or testimony that
   you will be introducing, prepare in advance and have a reason
   why you believe that evidence is admissible. Be ready to make
   that argument to the judge.
6) If the objection is to relevance, and you think you will be able to
   show that it is relevant after additional testimony, say to the
   judge, "I will connect it up in a few questions Your Honor."
   Such a statement is equivalent of saying "trust me." If you do
   say that, you had better connect it up later or else the judge will
   later strike your evidence and will not trust you in the future.

If You are a Judge Who Has to Rule on the Objection
1) If the specific objection was not identified, turn to the lawyer who made the objection and say, "Basis?" - Meaning, "What is the legal basis for your objection?"
2) After the lawyer has put their specific objection on the record, turn to the proponent (the lawyer who is attempting to introduce the evidence), and say, "What is your response?"
3) Allow more argument if necessary. "Counsel, how do you respond to that argument?"
4) After the arguments are completed, make your ruling.
   A) "Sustained" - meaning you agree with the objection, and you will exclude the evidence.
   B) "Overruled" - meaning you agree with the proponent of the evidence, and the evidence will be admissible.
   C) Reserve your ruling until the end of the trial. ("I will reserve my decision on this issue until the close of the testimony.")
   D) Ask lawyers to submit a written memorandum on the issue so you have a better understanding of the issue, the law, and the precedent.

Multiple Lawyers and Multiple Clients
If two or more lawyers represent one client, only one of the lawyers can object to each witness, e.g. if you do the direct, you are the only one who can object on cross. Co-counsel for the same party cannot both object or respond to objections for single witness. If there are multiple parties who each have their own lawyer, each lawyer must make their own objection to have the objections preserved for appeal.

Judges Apply the Rules of Evidence More Loosely in Nonjury Trials. Many jurisdictions seem to apply a presumption that a trial judge will ignore inadmissible evidence in a non-jury trial. Questionable evidence is very seldom basis for reversing a verdict in a nonjury trial.

The Key to Objections is Rule 103 There is a rhyme to this phrase. "Key" rhymes with "103." Rule 103 holds the key to understanding the process of objections. Read that rule very carefully. Almost all states have a rule similar to FRE 103.

FRE 103. Rulings on Evidence

(a) Preserving a Claim of Error. A party may claim error in a ruling to admit or exclude evidence only if the error affects a substantial right of the party and:

    (1) if the ruling admits evidence, a party, on the record:

        (A) timely objects or moves to strike; and

        (B) states the specific ground, unless it was apparent from the context; or

    (2) if the ruling excludes evidence, a party informs the court of its substance by an offer of proof, unless the substance was apparent from the context.

(b) Not Needing to Renew an Objection or Offer of Proof. Once the court rules definitively on the record — either before or at trial — a party need not renew an objection or offer of proof to preserve a claim of error for appeal.

(c) Court's Statement About the Ruling; Directing an Offer of Proof. The court may make any statement about the character or form of the evidence, the objection made, and the ruling. The court may direct that an offer of proof be made in question-and-answer form.

(d) Preventing the Jury from Hearing Inadmissible Evidence. To the extent practicable, the court must conduct a jury trial so that inadmissible evidence is not suggested to the jury by any means.

(e) Taking Notice of Plain Error. A court may take notice of a plain error affecting a substantial right, even if the claim of error was not properly preserved.

Important Points about Rule 103 include:

1) The objection must be timely and state the specific ground for the objection, unless it is apparent from the context.

2) If the evidence was admitted, appellate courts do not have to consider the issue unless a specific ground for the objection was timely stated.

3) If the evidence was excluded, the appellate court needs information about what the excluded evidence was going to be. That information must be provided by an "offer of proof" unless the information was apparent from the context.

4) The judge can make statements for the record about the objection, the evidence, the form of the evidence, the ruling, and can require an offer of proof in question and answer form.

5) An error is not sufficient to reverse the trial unless a "substantial right" of a party is affected.

6) Even if there was no objection at trial, "plain errors" affecting "substantial rights" can result in a reversal on appeal.

The Most Common Substantive Objections Are Based on The Rules of Evidence and Constitutional Issues. Each article within the evidence code has one or more common types of objections, such as:

	FRE
General provisions	100s
Objections	
Preliminary questions	
Limited admissibility	
Remainder of or related writings	
Judicial notice	200s
Presumptions	300s
Relevance	400s
Privileges	500s
Witnesses	600s
Competence	
Impeachment	
Opinions and expert testimony	700s
Hearsay	800s
Authentication	900s
Best evidence (original writings)	1000s

Motions in Limine

In a jury trial, a lawyer may make a pretrial motion in limine, which is a motion to exclude or admit certain evidence prior to trial. In jury trials, the motion is made outside the presence of the jury. The judge's ruling on the motion in limine can 1) prevent inadmissible evidence from being heard by a jury, or 2) allow lawyers to know that they can go forward and attempt to introduce certain evidence without risking a mistrial. Motions in limine are probably not necessary in a nonjury trial because the judge will have to hear the potentially inadmissible evidence before ruling on the motion. Therefore, even if the evidence would be ruled inadmissible, the trial judge who will be the trier of fact will have already heard the inadmissible evidence. Judges in nonjury trials are presumed to ignore inadmissible evidence.

Common Objections to the Form of the Question

Objections to the form of the question often have no clear answers or standards. Many judges and lawyers might disagree as to whether some question is improper or not. If a rule is cited when making the objection, it would usually be Rule 611.

Argumentative (also called **Harassing, Badgering**) **(R611)**
An argumentative question asks the witness to accept the examiner's summary, inference, or conclusion rather than a fact. Often the objector is trying to protect a witness during cross-examination.
Examples of Argumentative Questions:
"Isn't what you told this judge on its face ridiculous?"
"How can you expect the judge to believe that?"
"Are you telling this court that you don't know what a machete is?"
"Do you really expect the judge to believe that?"
"Do you mean to tell me…?"
"Doesn't it seem strange that…?"
"Your kind of the hatchet man down here for the D.A.s Office, aren't you?"
"It wouldn't bother you any, to come in here and lie from the time you started to the time you stopped, would it?"

Asked and Answered: This rule is violated by repeating the same question, asked by the same lawyer, to get the same answer, from the same witness. A question which has previously been asked and answered is being asked again. The rule prevents cumulative testimony R403. Similar questions are permitted if the identical information is not repeated. This objection does not apply to prevent the same questions being asked on cross-examination that were asked on direct examination by opposing counsel. It does not prevent asking identical questions of different witnesses, nor does it prevent a lawyer representing a co-party from asking the same questions to the same witness again.

Assuming Facts Not in Evidence. This rule is violated when part of a question (usually the first part) assumes the truth of a fact that is in dispute but has not yet been proved at trial. Such a question is unfair because it cannot be answered without conceding the unproven fact. Assuming facts not in evidence may be an attempt to bring into the trial information that the lawyer is not able to prove by other means. However, questions that assume facts are permitted on cross-examination to impeach a witness's credibility.

Examples of assuming facts not in evidence:

> "When did you stop beating your wife?" (assumes previous beatings)
>
> "Did you know their business dropped 50% because of what the defendant did?" (assumes the defendant did the same thing)
>
> "How long after you purchased the items were they given to the defendant?" (assumes the purchase)

Responses:

"I will connect it up later."(Which just means, "Judge trust me and allow a few more questions." If you request permission to "connect up later," you'd better be able to connect it up or the judge will no longer trust you.)

> "I have a good faith basis for assuming those facts. I would like to proceed without further tipping my hand."
>
> "This is criminal case and the defendant has a Sixth Amendment right to fully cross-examine the witness."

Beyond the Scope (of a prior direct of cross examination)

Questions on redirect examination cannot go into subject matters that have not been covered in the previous cross-examination. Similarly, questions on re-cross examination cannot go beyond the scope of redirect examination. Redirect examination is limited to issues raised by the opposing lawyer on cross-examination. If the questions go beyond the issues raised on cross, the objection will be valid.

Responses.

> "Your Honor, I'm allowed to go into this area because it goes to the witness's credibility."

Note well: Cross-examination is not limited to the subjects covered on direct examination. If it were so limited, the cross examiner would be prohibited from fully examining the witness and exposing weaknesses in the direct exam. If a "beyond the scope" objection is raised to a cross-examination question, the best response probably would be, "Your Honor, R611 allows me to cross on the subject matter of direct examination and "matters affecting the witness's credibility." My cross goes to credibility."

Compound Questions

A compound question has two or more separate questions in a single question, and usually contains the words "and" or "or." A simple "yes" or "no" answer to the question will be unclear. If the witness asked answers "yes" or "no," it is not clear if the "yes" or "no" applies to all the multiple parts of the question or just one part.

Examples:

"On that day, you went shopping <u>and</u> to the beach, didn't you?"

"Did you determine the time of death by interviewing witnesses <u>and</u> by requesting the autopsy report?"

"On Saturday, did you send the email <u>and</u> also call him?"

Cumulative (R403)

Cumulative questions ask for the same information from the same witness multiple times (like asked and answered) or ask multiple witnesses for the same information to establish the same facts.

Lack of (or insufficient) Foundation (R901)

A lack of foundation objection is proper when the lawyer asks a question before establishing the preliminary facts which would permit the questions. The evidence lacks testimony as to its authenticity or source.

Example:

"My partner saw Watkins stumble inside Cut-Rate Liquor store."

"Objection: Lack of personal knowledge – and hearsay."

Leading Question (R611)

A leading question improperly suggests the answer that the lawyer wants from the witness. Another definition is that a leading question contains the desired answer. The danger is that a leading question will make the witness agree with a false suggestion.

Often leading questions start with phrases like - "Isn't it true that... ""Did...?" or ends with "..., right?" Questions that start with the word "So" should be at least a yellow flag that the question might be leading. Although some questions are obviously leading, lawyers and judges often have different interpretations of what a leading question is. Be prepared to quickly rephrase your question if an objection to it is sustained to your question. Whether or not a question that contains the phrase <u>"whether or not"</u> is leading has been subject to much debate. A lawyer's nonverbal behavior or voice inflection is sometimes considered when determining whether a question is leading.

Leading is generally not permitted on direct examination. However, leading is allowed and in fact expected when cross examining a witness called by the opposing party.

Leading questions are permissible for preliminary matters, when a party calls a hostile witness or an adverse witness (FRE 611) or when a witness is very young, very old, or mentally challenged. Leading questions are also common and proper on direct examination when laying foundations because under FRE 104 the rules of evidence do not apply, except for privileges, when asking preliminary questions about the admissibility of evidence. Leading questions are also permissible when they are used like a topic sentence in a paragraph to move a witness on direct examination to another part of the scene. For example," Did there come a time when you went into the store?" Of course, the lawyer could get the same result by simply making the statement, "Now I want to ask you some questions about what you did when you went into the store." It is a common belief that the more a lawyer leads on direct examination, the less credibility the witness will have because the witness looks like they are being told what to say during the examination.

Motion to strike

Motions to strike are used two ways. First, Rule of Civil Procedure 12(f) allows for motions to strike certain pleadings. Second, Motions to strike, under evidence R103, are treated similarly to objections and ask the judge to strike inadmissible testimony from the record if the witness has just said the objectionable words. Of course, "striking" is not really striking. The inadmissible words are not removed from the court records but remain in the record even if the testimony is "stricken." The opposing lawyer can ask the judge to instruct the jury to disregard the "stricken" testimony, but psychologically, such an instruction to "disregard" the testimony might highlight the testimony for the jury. Tough choices to make.

Narrative Question, or Calls for A Narrative Answer, or simply Narrative Answer

A narrative objection can refer to a question that asks a witness to tell a story rather than to state only a few specific facts, or refer to a witness' answer which is several sentences, or even paragraphs, long. On one hand, narrative answers allow the witness to easily include inadmissible evidence, but on the other hand, a narrative story might more likely provide truthful facts.

Examples of narrative questions:

"What did you do that day?"

"Tell us about the accident."

"Now tell us what everyone said and did at that point."

"What happened that night?"

"How did the accident happen?"

Ans: "First thing I got up and I... Then I went to... After that I ... She told me that... And I immediately saw the ..."

Non-Responsive Answer: The non-responsive answer objection is made to an answer that does not answer the question that was asked. Simply, the witness does not answer the question asked by the lawyer. Often the witness is trying to make their own point and take control of the testimony. A problem with nonresponsive answers is that the witness is volunteering information that might be irrelevant or unfairly prejudicial. <u>In theory, only the lawyer asking the question can object to a non-responsive answer.</u> Some judges will only allow this objection from the lawyer who is asking the question. If the objection is sustained, it is often followed by a motion to strike the answer from the record. If the opposing lawyer is considering making a non-responsive answer objection, they should consider making some other appropriate objection such as "irrelevant," "unfairly prejudicial," or "lack of foundation."

Example of a non-responsive answers:

Q: "Did you see the other driver get out of his car right after the accident?"

A: "He told me he had insurance." (non-responsive)

Q: "Weren't you the last person the victim saw on the night of his death?"

A: "I had nothing to do with that!" (non-responsive)

Speculation – Calls for Speculation – Lack Person Knowledge. (R602)

A speculation objection is proper if the lawyer asks the witness a question that the witness has no personal knowledge about, or the witness testifies about something they have not perceived. A red flag signaling a call for speculation is often a question that starts with, Isn't it possible that…?" A better phrasing to accomplish the same objective would be to focus the question on the witness's personal knowledge and experience by asking for the same information but stating it as follows, "You don't know whether or not…, do you?"

Examples of a question calling for speculation:

"What do you think he was thinking about at that time?"

"Why would she do something like that?"

Vague and Ambiguous Question: Vague and ambiguous questions are asked in ways that are incomprehensible, incomplete, or the answer will be ambiguous. If you, as the opposing lawyer, do not understand the question asked by your opponent, then the witness probably does not understand the question either. Object.

Other Objections

Golden Rule

The Golden Rule objection is made when the opposing counsel places the trier of fact (judge or jury) in the same situation that the case is about.

Examples of a Golden Rule objection:

"Your Honor, what would you have done in a situation like that?"

"Ladies and gentlemen of the jury, would you want someone like that coming into your neighborhood?"

Speaking Objections

A speaking objection is a lawyer's attempt to influence the jury by speaking to the jury by using the objection. Although such objections are very disfavored by judges in jury trials, in nonjury trials such objections can be used to make an argument to the trial judge and influence the decision to be made on the objection.

Examples of speaking objections:

"Well Judge, I am going to strongly object to this procedure. I feel that I am being sandbagged here and I don't appreciate it."

"Your honor, it doesn't matter what the answer is. Opposing counsel just wants to make a statement. He doesn't care what this witness says."

Coaching the witness

Such objections can be used to communicate with and coach a witness.

Example of coaching the witness through an objection:

"Objection. The witness couldn't possibly know that answer."
Witness then responds by saying, "I don't know."

Relevance

Questions in a case about some other person, some other event, and some other time, are irrelevant unless the judge find such questions to be relevant in this particular case for a special reason such as to show bias or relevant in this case under Rule 404(b). I call such irrelevant evidence P.E.T. evidence and tell my students that PET evidence is not admissible - evidence about some other Person, or Event, or Time. Furthermore, questions about "**what most people do**" are almost always irrelevant.

Examples of irrelevant "what most people do" objections:

"Don't most people know that…?"

"Don't most people speed when their car is headed downhill?"

Evidentiary Foundations

Foundations - Predicates - Laying the Foundation

Foundations are questions asked by a lawyer to set the groundwork (the foundation) for admitting evidence at trial. The asking of these questions is often referred to as "**laying the foundation**" for the evidence. The word "**predicates,**" when used by trial lawyers, refers to a series of form or sample questions that a lawyer must ask to establish the facts, events, or conditions which are required by the rules of evidence or caselaw before presenting other evidence. Predicates are the questions that are asked when laying the foundation for other evidence. The evidentiary foundation is like the foundation for a building. It provides a solid basis for building up the structure of the case at trial. The necessary foundational questions are not always obvious by reading the rules of evidence.

Foundations may come from local legal culture - "That's the way we do things in this jurisdiction," or from a lawyer or judge's prior experience - "That's the way I was taught to do it," or "That's what I think works best," or "That's what I am requiring you to do."

Bare-Bones Foundations

The foundations provided in this book are designed to be brief - what I call "bare-bones foundations." A "**bare-bones**" foundation uses the minimum necessary questions to admit a piece of evidence or testimony and is less concerned about the "weight" of the evidence to be admitted. Bare-bones foundations are commonly used in non-jury trials. On the other hand, what I call "**advocacy foundations**" are more common in jury trials where a jury of laypeople will make the important factual determinations in the case. An advocacy foundation uses more than the bare minimum number of questions to lay the foundation, with additional questions going to enhance the persuasiveness of the sponsoring witness and the evidence.

For example, when using a police officer's report to refresh memory, or for recorded recollection, or to impeach, the additional questions might include questions relating to the training or conduct of the officer, such as:

"Did you have training in writing reports?"

"How much training?"

"When you are writing your report, you knew that your supervisor will read some of your reports?"

"You know that your future assignments might depend on the quality of your written reports?"

"Do you reread your report before submitting it?"

"Do you check your report for accuracy before submitting it?"

Steps for Introducing Exhibits

Preliminary steps are:

1) Have the exhibit marked for identification
2) Show the proposed exhibit to opposing counsel
3) Ask permission to approach the witness with the proposed exhibit

---

1. History - How the witness knows the exhibit.

Offer some testimony that the witness <u>knows</u> or is <u>familiar with</u> the evidence – such as a document, physical item, photo, diagram, scene, text message, email - or recalls the statement. Even if the witness has only seen the exhibit once before or has just been to the scene shown in the photograph once before, <u>once is enough</u>.

2. The litany (a ritualistic repetition of foundational questions)

a) **Ask the court clerk to mark the item** (using numbers or letters). The clerk will decide which system to use. In more serious cases in the jurisdiction's higher courts (typically where jury trials are allowed), exhibits are usually required to be marked at least before trial starts, and often during pretrial conferences.

b) **Show opposing counsel** (this will prevent interruptions) and say, "Let the record reflect that I am showing the defense what has been marked as plaintiff's proposed exhibit number one."

c) **Ask the judge for permission to approach the witness**. "May I approach the witness?"

- Q: **"I show you what has been marked as** Plaintiff's (Prosecution's) (Defense's) proposed exhibit # x (or exhibit #x for identification purposes) **and ask whether you can identify it"** (You expect a "yes" answer here.)

- Q: **"What is it?"** (They describe it in general terms. "It is the contract/photo of the scene/weapon recovered/drugs seized/diagram of the area/etc.")

- Q: **"How do you know that?"** ("I recognize it. It has my signature on it. / I have been there many times before. / I put my initials on it and the defendant's name/etc.")

3. Show Condition or Comparison or Accuracy

Some comparison must be made between the exhibit in court and when the witness became familiar with the exhibit out-of-court. Of the examples that follow, only one such question is necessary.

- "Is this in the **same condition** as when you... [first saw it...seized it...etc.]?"
- "Is this in the **same or substantially** the same condition.... as when you..." (for item or document)
- "Is it a **fair and accurate representation** of the X **as it was that day**?" (for diagram or pictures)
- "**Has it changed** in any significant way?"
- "**How does it compare** to the item you saw that day?"

4. Move or Offer the Exhibit into Evidence

"Your honor, **I offer the exhibit into evidence**."

- or, "I move the exhibit into evidence."

You could instead say, "I offer proposed exhibit # 1 into evidence as exhibit # 1," but why make it so confusing? Just say, "I offer the exhibit into evidence."

The judge <u>might</u> ask the opposing counsel, "Any objections?"

but if there is an objection to the admissibility (not the weight), the opponent should object immediately after the proponent offers the exhibit.

The judge should allow "voir dire" (immediate cross examination limited to the foundation and the admissibility) by the opponent of the exhibit.

The Common Evidentiary Foundations

(You should be able to do all of these in your sleep)

Physical Items
Photograph (printed)
Diagram of scene
Physical item seized at scene

Common Documents
Refreshing memory
Recorded recollection
Business records in paper
Business records – and self-authentication under R902
Deposition impeachment (see below)

Records and Treatises
Public record
Learned treatise –
     Use on direct supporting your expert
     Use on cross attacking their expert

Digital Evidence – from the internet, a cell phone, or a computer
Also called - ESI – Electronically Stored Information
Emails
Text message – issues of incompleteness
Social Media - Facebook, Instagram, Twitter, Snapchat
Website posting
Voicemail recording
Videos, including on cell phone
Photo on cell phone
Fax
Chatroom conversations

Impeachment
     Impeaching by Prior Written Inconsistent statement
     Impeaching by Omission in Prior Written Statement
     Impeaching by Prior Oral Inconsistent statement
     Impeaching by Inconsistent Oral Deposition Transcript

Phrases to Move Evidence into a Trial

(Pick one and always use it)

"I offer the exhibit into evidence." (By far the easiest to use)

"Your Honor, I ask that what's been previously marked as Plaintiff's Exhibit A for Identification be admitted into evidence as Plaintiff's A." (Unnecessarily complex and you are likely to mess it up.)

"At this time, we offer Plaintiff's A for identification into evidence as Plaintiff's exhibit A."

"The Government at this time, would move to introduce Government's Exhibit No. 2 into evidence."

"Your Honor, we'd offer Defense Exhibit B into evidence."

"Your Honor, I move that Plaintiff's Exhibit 3 be introduced into evidence."

"We offer Exhibit A into evidence."

"Your Honor, I would like to submit People's exhibit 'A' into evidence."

"We would ask the Court to admit State's Exhibit 4 for Identification as State's 4."

Useful Points to Remember

Offering something "into evidence" means that in a jury trial the exhibit can go into the jury room and be reviewed as many times as the jurors want to look at it.

Make an Offer of Proof – if your evidence is not admitted. R103.

Hearsay within hearsay – statements incorporated into other statements need an additional hearsay exception to be admissible. R805 Hearsay Within Hearsay.

Public records do not have to be "open to the public" but rather are reports and records created by public (government) employees. R803(8)

A record automatically generated by a computer - is not hearsay (computer generated records). No assertion by a person.

Email offered to show notice, knowledge, or fear are not assertions and therefore not hearsay. In a contract or consent form, the words have independent legal significance, which means they operate to form a contract even if they are not true.

Demonstrative evidence – demonstrates or represents some real evidence. Also sometimes called **illustrative evidence**, as compared to **real evidence**, which as some historical connection to the case - such as being the drugs, the gun, etc.

A "chain of custody" is required for fungible items that cannot be identified and distinguished on sight, such as drugs, alcohol, and blood samples. They are as indistinguishable as grains of sand. Often, they are taken into custody and sent to a laboratory for testing. The "chain" makes sure the evidence that is tested is connected to the correct case.

Distinctive characteristics. Evidence tags with initials and case names make items unique and should qualify as a **"Distinctive characteristic"** under R901(b)(4) for authentication purposes.

The most common methods to introduce physical and documentary evidence are **using personal knowledge and distinctive characteristics.** R901(b)(1)&(4)

Affidavits are hearsay and not admissible at trial. However, affidavits can be used in summary judgment proceedings if the statements in the affidavits would be admissible in court if testified to by the declarant with personal knowledge. Therefore, lawyers should not be sign affidavits for summary judgement. Potential witnesses with personal knowledge of the facts must sign the affidavits.

HARROWing - a Barkai mnemonic/acronym formed from the first letters of evidence concepts most likely to impact admissibility decisions. Always think of HARROWing when a physical item is going to be introduced, especially if the item is a document or a physical item with words on it. **H**earsay R800s, **A**uthentication R900s, **R**elevance R401, **R**elevance R403, **O**riginal **W**ritings (Best Evidence) R1000s. HARROWing also applies to ESI (Electronically Stored Information) such as emails, texts, websites, etc.

OTP - what is the evidence "Offered to Prove?" OTP impacts relevance, admissibility, and the necessary foundation.

The rules of evidence do not tell you how to introduce exhibits although some rules do list the foundational elements which must be included in foundational questions. The hearsay exceptions of Recorded Recollection R803(5) and Records of a Regular Conducted Activity (business records) R803(6) are examples of hearsay exceptions that are so complicated that a novice trial lawyer might want to have the rule in front of them when attempting to lay the foundation.

Laying a foundation is like a sport. Practice before the game.

Steps: Mark/Pre-Mark, Show, Approach, Foundational Questions, Offer
> **Mark exhibits.** Have the exhibit marked before trial or prior to trial – depending on the court rules.

Magic Words: "<u>**in the same or substantially the same condition**</u>" or "<u>**fair and accurate representation**</u>," or "<u>**fairly accurate representation**</u>," or "<u>**fairly represent**</u>."

Speak in generic terms when talking about exhibits until the witness identifies the exhibit: "<u>Proposed exhibit # 1</u>" or "<u>Exhibit # 1 for identification purposes</u>," not "Your report," or "Photo of the scene."

To "<u>publish</u>" an exhibit means to show the exhibit to the jury or ask the judge to look at the exhibit right now, not at the end of the trial.

Chain of evidence is usually only necessary for fungible items (identical items; they all look the same), or items that need testing – drugs, alcohol, blood, DNA. Not every "kink in the link" of the chain of evidence makes evidence inadmissible. Authentication only requires production of evidence "sufficient to support a finding," R901(a)(1), which is a low standard.

Basic tasks that every trial lawyer should be able to do
- introduce documents, physical items, photographs
- refresh memory (almost always done on direct)
- use the recollection recorded hearsay exception (almost always done on direct).
- impeach (almost always done on cross); inconsistent statements & omissions.

The Best Foundation Resources
- Grimm, Joseph & Capra, Best Practices for Authenticating Digital Evidence 69 Baylor L Rev. 1 (2017)
- Evidentiary Foundations for Government Attorneys (2015) (from National Attorneys General Training & Research Institute) - (JB: It contains many simple foundations.)
- Edward Imwinkelried, Evidentiary Foundations, (10th ed. 2018) – (The classic source for foundations, but less than you might want about ESI foundations, and more than you might want in the middle of trial.)
- Deanne Siemer, Laying Foundations and Meeting Objections (4th ed. 2013)

Important Evidence Rules to Guide You

FRE 103(c) Directing an Offer of Proof. – explains how to protect the record for appeal if your evidence is excluded at trial.

FRE 104 Preliminary questions.
(a) In General. In [deciding preliminary questions] the court is <u>not bound by evidence rules</u> except those on privilege.
    [**Barkai says:** that means <u>you can lead on direct for foundations.</u>]
(b) Relevance that Depends on a Fact. When the relevance of evidence depends on whether a fact exists, proof must be introduced <u>sufficient to support a finding</u> that the fact does exist.
    [**Barkai says:** <u>that is a low threshold.</u>]

FRE 901 Authenticating or Identifying Evidence.
(a) In General. To satisfy the requirement of authenticating or identifying an item of evidence, the proponent must produce <u>evidence sufficient to support a finding</u> that the item is what the proponent claims it is. [**Barkai says:** <u>that is a low threshold</u>]
(b) Examples. The following are examples only —
    (1) Testimony of a Witness with Knowledge. Testimony that an item is what it is claimed to be.
    (4) Distinctive Characteristics and the Like. The appearance, contents, substance, internal patterns, or other <u>distinctive characteristics</u> of the item, <u>taken together with all the circumstances.</u>
    (7) Evidence About Public Records.
    (9) Evidence About a Process or System.

FRE 612 Writing Used to Refresh a Witness's Memory. Witness does not need to be the author. Anything can be used to refresh memory - even "my left shoe," which is my in-class example.

FRE 613 Witness's Prior Statement. Impeachment by inconsistent statements and omissions.

FRE 801(d)(1) Not Hearsay: A Declarant-Witness's Prior Statement. (Inconsistent under oath, consistent, or prior ID)

FRE 803(6) Records of a Regularly Conducted Activity (JB: <u>business records are **KRAP**</u>**)**
    (**K**ept in the course, **R**egular practice, **A**t or near the time, **P**ersonal knowledge)

FRE 902 Evidence That Is Self-Authenticating

902(11) Certified Domestic Records of a Regularly Conducted Activity. [Note: There are many certification forms available on the internet. At least 32 states have adopted this 2002 FRE amendment.]

902(13) Certified Records Generated by an Electronic Process or System. [Only 10 states had adopted this 2017 FRE amendment.]

902(14) Certified Data Copied from an Electronic Device, Storage Medium, or File. [Only 10 states had adopted this 2017 FRE amendment.]

R105 Limited Admissibility (admitted against only one party or for a limited purpose)
Only 3 states and the District of Columbia have no rule or statute similar to R105 and rely on case law (Massachusetts, Missouri, and New York).

R106 Remainder of / related writing [Barkai says this means to admit the remainder now]. Only 4 states have no rule or statute (Kansas, Massachusetts, Missouri, and New York).

R1006 Summaries…voluminous writings which cannot conveniently be examined in court.

The Opponent Has the Burden
On the Issue of Trustworthiness of Records

Since this 2014 FRE amendment, the burden of showing a record lacks trustworthiness is on the opponent in the Federal rules – FRE 803(6)(7)(8) …"and, the opponent does not show …a lack of trustworthiness."

8 states have also amended their rules placing the burden of showing that the source of the source of information or other circumstances indicate a lack of trustworthiness on the opponent (Arizona, Mississippi, New Hampshire, New Mexico, Oregon, South Dakota, Utah, and West Virginia).

Basic Foundations & Impeachment Examples

Several of the following foundation and impeachment examples are based upon the facts of

NITA Liquor Commission v. Cut-Rate Liquor and Jones*

In this famous, fictional case from NITA (National Institute of Trial Advocacy), Walter Watkins was observed going into the Cut-Rate Liquor Store by Officer Bier and his partner from their unmarked car which was parked across the street from the liquor store. The officers had a partial view into the store and saw Watkins appear to purchase liquor at the counter. Watkins was arrested outside the store as he was leaving with a brown paper bag which contained a bottle of Thunderbird Wine. Cut-Rate Liquors and the clerk Dan Jones were issued citations for selling liquor to a person under the influence of liquor.

* This NITA Liquor Problem is used with the permission of the National Institute of Trial Advocacy (NITA). The terms "Officer Bier, Thunderbird Wine, Jackson & 7th Street, April 5th, Walter Watkins, and shoulders up" used in this publication are original to the Nita Liquor Commission v. Cut-Rate Liquor and Jones problem from *Problems in Trial Advocacy* by Donald H. Beskind and Anthony J. Bocchino, published by the National Institute of Trial Advocacy. The basis of the NITA Liquor problem and the specified terms are used here with permission.

NITA Liquor Commission
v.
Jones

The Facts

This case is a civil action brought by the Liquor Commission against Dan Jones and the Cut-Rate Liquor Store for civil penalties, including possible revocation of Cut-Rate's liquor license. Investigator Bier is a typical investigator-police officer and has investigated many such incidents. Bier's official report appears on the next page along with a diagram of the scene.

Dan Jones and the Cut-Rate Liquor Store deny that Watkins was intoxicated on the evening of April 5 when he was in their store. Jones says that Watkins did not appear to be intoxicated when he observed Watkins in the store. Watkins was convicted of public intoxication at a prior trial. Watkins is not present for this Cut-Rate case.

1. Prepare to do a direct examination of Officer Bier for the government.

2. Prepare to do a cross examination of Officer Bier for the Defense.

Officer Bier's Report

NITA LIQUOR COMMISSION OFFICIAL REPORT

My partner Donald Smith and I are investigators for the Nita Liquor Commission. On the evening of April 5, at approximately 8:45 p.m., we were parked near the Cut-Rate Liquor Store when we observed an individual, later identified as Walter Watkins, attempting to cross 7th Street. Mr. Watkins was staggering and had great difficulty making it to the other side of the street. He stumbled and almost fell at the curb on the south side of 7th Street. He walked to the entrance of the Cut-Rate Liquor Store, and then paused for a few moments before he entered the store. The front of the store had a plate glass window with displays and advertising in it. From our car, we could see Mr. Watkins from the shoulders up through the window. We observed Mr. Watkins approach the counter and say a few words to the clerk, Dan Jones. A few minutes later, Watkins emerged from the store carrying a bottle of Thunderbird wine in a brown paper sack.

I stopped Mr. Watkins as he exited the store. I detected the odor of alcohol and administered a field sobriety test. I then arrested Watkins and issued him a citation for public intoxication, seized the wine, and issued a citation to Dan Jones and the Cut-Rate Liquor store for violation of H.R.S. 281-78 which contains the following language:

> No licensee nor its employees shall sell or furnish any liquor to any person at the time under the influence of liquor.

I have attached a diagram of the scene to this report.

Date: April 5   Time: 22:15

signed J. Bier

_____

Diagram of Cut-Rate Liquor Store Area

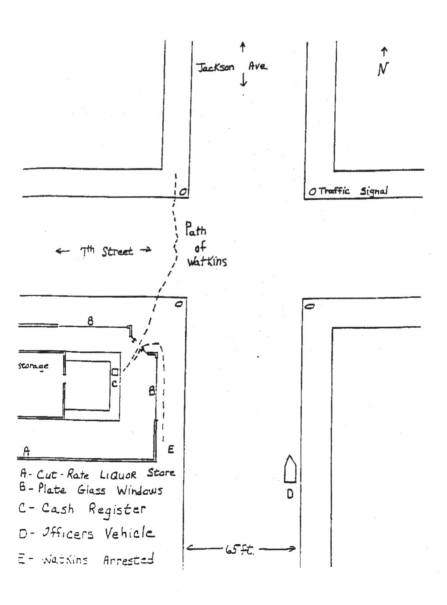

Jackson Ave.

N

O Traffic Signal

Path
of
Watkins

← 7th Street →

B

storage

C

B

A

E

A - Cut-Rate Liquor Store
B - Plate Glass Windows
C - Cash Register
D - Officers Vehicle
E - Watkins Arrested

D

← 65 ft. →

Photograph of a Scene

Introduce a photograph of Cut-Rate Liquor Store where the clerk and the liquor store were charged with selling liquor to an intoxicated person. R901(B)(1) (Testimony of a Witness with Knowledge)

Q: Officer Bier, where were you on the night of April 5?
A: Parked in an unmark car outside Cut-Rate Liquor Store.

Q: Let me show you what has been marked as Plaintiff's proposed exhibit # 1.   <u>What is it?</u>
A: It is a photograph of Cut-Rate Liquor Store where I was parked on April 5th.

Q: <u>How do you know that?</u>
A: I was at the store that night. I recognize it. I took the photo.

Q: Is the photograph a <u>fair and accurate representation</u> of Cut-Rate Liquor store as it appeared <u>on April 5th</u>?
A: Yes.

Q: Your Honor, I offer the exhibit into evidence.

Enhancements/Additional Questions
- "Please describe the appearance of the store."
- "How many times have you seen the Cut-Rate Liquor Store?"
     (Ask this question only if the witness has been to the store many times. However, being there once is enough for the foundation.) The witness can authenticate the photo even if the trial event was the only time the witness ever saw the store pictured in the photo

Additional Points:
- The photographer is not a necessary witness.
- The witness's personal knowledge of the contents of the photograph is all that is necessary.
- The witness does not have to have seen the photograph before coming to court.
- Print the photo and bring copies to court for the judge, jury, and opposing counsel.
- The photo could be a "Street view" from Google Maps that the witness has never seen before.

Diagram of the Scene

Demonstrative Evidence

Diagram from Officer Bier's Report

After some testimony about the events.

Q: Officer Bier, did you make a diagram of the scene that night? (Ans: Yes)

Q: Let me show you what has been marked as Plaintiff's proposed exhibit # 1. <u>What is it?</u> (Ans: My diagram)

Q: <u>How do you know that?</u> (Ans: I drew it. I remember it. That's my writing)

Q: Is it a <u>fair and accurate representation</u> of the intersection of Jackson and 7th Streets <u>on April 5th</u>? (Ans: Yes.)

Q: Is the proposed exhibit in the <u>same condition</u> as it was when you drew it on April 5th? (Ans: Yes.)

Q: Your Honor, I offer the exhibit into evidence.

Real Evidence

The Bottle of Thunderbird Wine Seized by Officer Bier

After some testimony about the events.

Q: Officer Bier, <u>what, if anything, did you recover</u> from Mr. Watkins that night?
       (Ans: A bottle and a bag)

Q: Let me hand you what has been marked as Plaintiff's proposed exhibit # 2. <u>What is it?</u>
       (Ans: The bottle and bag I seized from Watkins)

       [If the bottle is in a bag, leave it in the bag. Have both the bottle and bag marked separately, e.g., Exhibits 1 and 2, A and B, 1 and 1A. Let the witness take the bottle out of the bag, like unwrapping a present. It will create some interest in what might be an otherwise boring trial.]

Q: <u>How do you know that?</u>
       [Ans: My initials, in my handwriting, are on the bag along with the words "Cut-Rate Liquor" and "April 5."]

Q: Is the proposed exhibit # 2 <u>in the same or substantially the same condition</u> as it was when you recovered it from Watkins on April 5th?
       (Ans: Generally, yes. However, some of the liquid was removed for testing for alcohol.)

Q: Your Honor, I offer the exhibit into evidence.

Offering A Contract into Evidence

Q: Mr. Johnny, I now want to ask you some questions about your dealings with Mr. King. In September, two years ago, did you have several conversations with Mr. King?

A: Yes. I did.

Q: What was the result of those conversations?

A: Mr. King and I entered into a contract for legal work.

Assume the exhibit has been pre-<u>marked</u> before the day of trial

Q: Let the record reflect that I am <u>handing</u> Mr. Johnny what has been pre-marked, as required by Court Rule, Plaintiff's proposed Exhibit # 1.
<u>What is it Mr. Johnny?</u>

A: It's the contract between me and Mr. King for the legal work that I was going to do for him.

Q: <u>How do you know that?</u> [Prepare the witness to answer this question]

A: I drafted this contract. I recognize it. That's my signature on it as well as Mr. King's.

Q: Is the contract in the <u>same condition</u> as it was two years when you both signed it.

A: Yes. There are no alterations to the contract.

Q: You Honor, I <u>offer</u> the exhibit into evidence

Writing Used to Refresh Memory

If a writing was used to refresh memory, R612 allows

as a matter of right, if the document was used in court;
with judge's discretion, if the document was used out of court

the opponent to:

1) see the writing in court,
2) inspect it
3) cross-examine on it, and
4) introduce portions of it (related to the testimony)

Simply: **Get (produced), Inspect, Cross, Introduce.**

However, it would be very unusual for an opponent to introduce the document because most of the document would hurt the opponent's case. If the opponent wanted to introduce only portions of the document, the lawyer who used it to refresh memory would have an argument that under R106, in fairness other parts of the document should be considered at the same time.

Rule 612. Writing used to refresh memory. (paraphrased)
   If a witness uses a writing to refresh memory for the purpose of testifying, either:
   (1) while testifying; or
   (2) before testifying, if the court in its discretion determines it is necessary in the interests of justice,
   an adverse party is entitled
   to have the writing produced at the hearing,
   to inspect it,
   to cross-examine the witness thereon, and
   to introduce in evidence those portions which relate to the
      testimony of the witness.

Refreshing Memory
with a Leading Question

(Using the same facts as the previous example)

Q: Do you recall anything else about Watkins as he crossed the
    street.
A: Not really

Q: Did he stumble and almost fall?

Opposing Lawyer: Objection: Leading

Q: I'll rephrase my question. What else do you recall about Watkins
    as he crossed the street.
A: Now I recall that he did stumble and almost fell crossing the
    street. I'm nervous. I forgot.

Note: The witness's credibility might have decreased somewhat
      because of the leading question, but the lawyer got the answer
      that was needed. The less important the information, the more
      likely leading will have little or no impact on your case.

Leading on Minor Issues
When the Witness Has Gone Off Course

Q: What day of the week did this happen?
A: Tuesday.

Q: You said Tuesday. Did you actually mean Monday?
A: Oh right, sorry. It was Monday.

Recorded Recollection (Author's Rule)

Recorded recollection is a hearsay exception that allows <u>for reading into evidence</u> a statement that was made by a witness on the stand who can no longer recall the facts even after there has been attempts to refresh the witness's memory. Recorded recollection is <u>almost always done on direct examination</u> with a witness the lawyer has called to testify. This foundation is complicated and not intuitive.

In the NITA problem, assume that attempts to refresh the witness's memory did not work. Therefore, assume the previous question and answer were:

Q: What else do you now recall?
A: Sorry, I truly do not remember any more.

[Lawyer now moves into the foundation for Recorded Recollection, under R803(5).

Q: Let me again show you proposed exhibit # 3. That is your report of this incident, right? (Note: Leading is appropriate when establishing any foundations under FRE 104(a) and similar state rules).
A: Yes

Q: You made that report when the incident was <u>fresh</u> in your mind?
A: Yes, just about an hour after the incident.

Q: Does the report <u>accurately reflect your knowledge</u> of the incident at the time of the incident?
A: Yes.

Q: Although you <u>once knew the details</u> of the incident and wrote them in your report, right now <u>you cannot now recall</u> the details of the incident well enough <u>to testify fully and accurately</u>, right?
A: Yes.

Q: Your honor, I would now <u>like to read</u> into the record those parts of the report that the witness no longer remembers. [Or, you could ask to have the witness read the portions of the report.]

(Discussion continued on the next page)

FRE 803(5) Recorded Recollection A record that:
    (A) is on a matter the witness once knew about but now cannot recall well enough to testify fully and accurately;
    (B) was made or adopted by the witness when the matter was fresh in the witness's memory; and
    (C) accurately reflects the witness's knowledge.
    If admitted, the record may be read into evidence but may be received as an exhibit only if offered by an adverse party.

Additional Points: "Admission" into evidence comes from reading parts of the document into evidence. The document is not physically admitted by the proponent of the evidence. It cannot be taken into the jury room. Information in this hearsay document is admitted (heard) only once like oral testimony. Also, admitting information from a "Learned Treatise" under that hearsay exception R803(18) is a similar process in that the information from the treatise can only be read and not physically introduced.

Almost always, the witness was the author of the document used as the recorded recollection. Refreshing memory under R612 and recorded recollection are almost always done on direct examination. Witnesses are impeached on cross, not refreshed. You would not normally use recorded recollection on cross because almost all of the document goes against your client.

    I think most lawyers prefer to read the recollection on direct examination themselves and not have the witness read it. By reading the recollection yourself, you can add what you consider the best tone, volume, pace, and emphasis for your case. Remember, when you use a past recollection recorded with your witness on direct, you cannot physically introduce the document into evidence. The proponent of the past recollection recorded "admits" the recollection by reading it, not physically admitting it.

    Recorded recollection documents are not business records. Business records do get admitted into evidence. The difference is that if admitted, the evidence can be taken into the jury room and be consulted by the jury many times during deliberations.

    A past recollection recorded includes all notes that a witness makes on any type of document. In evidence class, I pull out my wallet and show students all the recorded recollections that I have in my wallet (post-it notes, notes on business cards, notes on little scraps of paper, etc.) and any notes I have taken on my cell phone. Recorded Recollections and Statements in Learned Treatises under R803(18) are two types of hearsay documents which can only be read into evidence but not physically introduced, at least not by the proponent of a recorded recollection.

Business Records - Custodian of Records
(The actual hearsay exception is for "Regularly Conducted Activity," but is usually called "Business Records")

To prove that Cut-Rate Liquors had Thunderbird Wine in stock on April 5, a business record can be offered.

Q: Please state your name, occupation, and why you are here today.

A: I am Mr. Data, an employee of Cut-Rate Liquors. My duties at Cut-Rate include serving as the custodian of business inventory records for Cut-Rate. I am here today pursuant to a subpoena to bring inventory records of Cut-Rate for April 5th.

Q: Did you bring with you today a copy of the Cut-Rate inventory records pertaining to Thunderbird wine for April 5th with you?

A: Yes.

Q: Do you know how Cut-Rate maintains its inventory records?

A: Yes.

Q: I show you what has been pre-marked as proposed exhibit # 1 and ask if you can identify what it is?

A: Yes, I can. Those are the Cute-Rate inventory records that I brought to court.

Q: Are those inventory records made by a person with <u>personal knowledge</u>, <u>at or near the time</u> the inventory is taken?

A: Yes.

Q: Are those records <u>kept in the course of a regularly conducted activity</u> of a business?

A: Yes.

Q: Is making those records a <u>regular practice</u> of Cut-Rate's business?

A: Yes.

Q: Your Honor, I offer the exhibit into evidence.

Publishing a Business Record: After being admitted, the business record can be "published" (which means it can be shown to the trier to fact). Depending on the judge's practice, the lawyer might be able to have the information from the record read to jury when it is admitted. If so, the Q & A could be:

Q: What do those records say about whether Cut-Rate had Thunderbird Wine in stock on April 5th?

A: "Thunderbird Wine, quantity 5," which means that Cut-Rate had five bottles of Thunderbird Wine in stock on April 5.

Remember, **business records are KRAP**. That mnemonic always gets my students' attention, and it helps them remember the foundation's components. **KRAP** – means:
<u>K</u>ept in the course,
<u>R</u>egular practice,
<u>A</u>t or near the time,
<u>P</u>ersonal knowledge

The **custodian of records or other qualified witness** required by the business record evidence rule is often the owner of the business, a bookkeeper, or anybody who works in the business. They just have to be able to answer questions to provide the appropriate foundation.

Although it adds to the weight of the evidence to have a witness who has been employed for many years in the data collection of the business, that is not required. The custodian only needs to be able to testify to the foundation requirements. The custodian could have only been the custodian for one day, if they can credibly answer the foundational questions (although that fact might go to the weight of the evidence, but not its admissibility). The custodian does not have to be employed on the day the record was made.

I would prefer to use a self-authenticating business record. The custodian is open to a difficult cross.
"Do you know who made the business entry?" – Know their work history? Have they been disciplined? Know their accuracy? Are they still with the company? (Of course, you need a good faith basis to ask such cross questions).

Impeachment by Prior Written Inconsistent Statement
FRE 613

Impeach Officer Bier from his report in the NITA problem, assuming Bier testified on direct exam, "I saw Watkins from the waist up inside the store."

> Direct exam testimony was "...from the <u>waist</u> up...."
>
> Report says "...from the <u>shoulders</u> up..."

Q: T<u>oday</u> you testified on direct examination[1] that you could see Watkins inside the store from the <u>waist up</u>? (said in a disbelieving tone) (Commit to today's testimony.)

A: Yes.

Q: You made a written report in this case within a few hours of the incident? (Credit prior statement's reliability)

A: Yes.

Q: Let the record reflect that I am handing the witness proposed exhibit #x. Mr. Bier, proposed exhibit #x is the report you made within a couple of hours after the incident?

A: Yes.

Q: That is your signature on the report?

A: Yes

Q: Even though you said on direct examination that you could see Mr. Watkins inside the store from the waist up, doesn't it say right here in your report (pointing to it) that "we could see Mr. Watkins from the <u>shoulders up</u> through the window"?

A: Yes.

(Discussion continued on the next page)

---

[1] I suggest that you only use the phrase – "You testified on direct" – when you are going to impeach a witness with a prior statement. Do not use that phrase when you are asking questions about a real event that took place in your case. What happened on the day of the incident might be different than what a witness testified to on direct. You should keep the trier of fact's attention on the incident itself, not the testimony on direct – unless you are impeaching that direct testimony.

Stop. Ask no further questions on this topic. Don't say, "Are you lying today or were you lying then?" Such a question is probably argumentative and objectionable anyway. Do not argue with the witness or ask the witness to admit they are not telling the truth. Save the credibility argument for closing argument. In closing argument, you can make an argument without having the witness trying to explain away your impeachment.

Understand the difference between testimony about "waist up" and "shoulders up." If Officer Bier could see Mr. Watkins inside the store from the waist up, he could have seen the bottle of wine, the cash register, any money changing hands, and the wine bottle changing hands. All those facts go to showing that there was a sale of wine in violation of the statute. However, if the officer could only see inside the store at the shoulders up level, then he was not able to see any direct sale and the defense has a better argument.

Three impeaching steps here: commit; credit; and confront. 1) Commit the witness to the statement made on direct, 2) credit the prior out-of-court statement, and 3) confront the witness with the difference.

By putting the conflicting statements in one sentence by using a dependent clause ("Even though you said on direct examination that…"), the trier of fact cannot miss the contradiction. Some impeaching lawyers will emphasize certain words in their questions, so the trier of fact does not miss the inconsistency. For example, they would emphasize with tone, volume, pace, and any other nonverbal's, the words "waist up" and "shoulder up." The impeaching lawyer might want to make eye contact with the judge or the jury when emphasizing those words.

Additional questions that are sometimes asked, especially if it is a jury trial:

> Your prior statement was made closer in time to the event than your statement today?
> Your memory was better at the earlier time?
> You have had training on how to write reports?
> You know that your supervisor will read your reports?
> You know that you are evaluated on, and perhaps even promoted or demoted based on the quality of your reports?

Impeachment by Omission

Assume that <u>Bier testified on direct exam</u>, "As I was sitting in my car watching Watkins <u>inside the store, I saw that Watkins stumble and almost fall as he approached the counter.</u>" However, Officer Bier's report does not say that Watkins stumbled and almost fell inside the store. In fact, the report indicates that the officer could only see Watkins from the shoulders up as he approached the counter. Impeachment by omission - meaning that the witness testified in court to something that was not in the report - it is a little harder to accomplish than a direct prior inconsistent statement, but it is still very doable.

Q: <u>You testified on direct</u> examination that you saw Mr. Watkins stumble and almost fall as he approached the counter inside from the store? (Credit prior statement's reliability)

A: Yes.

Q: You made a written report in this case within an hour of the incident, right?

A: Yes.

Q: I am handing the witness proposed exhibit #x.
    This is the report you made within a couple of hours after the incident, isn't it?

A: Yes.

Q: That is your signature on the report, isn't that true?

A: Yes

Q: <u>Even though you said on direct examination</u> that you saw Mr. Watkins <u>stumble and almost fall</u> as he approached the counter <u>inside</u> the store, <u>nowhere</u> in this report that you prepared <u>does it state</u> that you saw Watkins stumble and almost fall <u>inside</u> the store, does it? [If the witness takes time to look for it in the report, give them as much time as they want to take.

A: No, it doesn't say that.

The report says nothing about Watkins' behavior in the store. Behavior in the store is critical to proving that defendant Jones knew that Watkins was intoxicated.

Additional questions beyond the bare-bones foundation.
　　Lawyer could build up the report, for example:

> "You try to put everything that is important in the report, right?"
> "They taught you to do that in the department training, right?"

The potential re-direct examination:
If it were my witness who was impeached, my redirect would go something like this:
　　Q: Officer, how do you explain what seems to be an inconsistency between your direct testimony that Watkins stumbled inside the store and your report, which does not mention Watkins stumbled inside the store?
　　A: [Perhaps the best answer would be] I can't put everything into the report. But I clearly remember that he stumbled inside the store.

Impeachment by Inconsistent Oral Deposition

Assume the same factual inconsistency of testimony on direct examination that Mr. Watkins stumbled inside the store, but this time also assume that Officer Bier gave an oral deposition under oath and gave an answer that did not mention any stumbling inside the store.

After laying a foundation which would include the procedures involved in the deposition, such as:
- You came to my office?
- You took an oath to tell the truth?
- I told you that if you didn't understand the question, you should tell me you don't understand?
- You had an opportunity to review and correct the transcript some weeks after the deposition?
- After you read the typed deposition, you signed the deposition as being accurate?

then complete the impeachment by reading the questions that were asked and the answers that were given at the deposition.

The impeaching sequence could go something like this:

Q: Even though you said on direct that Watkins stumbled and almost fell in the store when he was at the counter, at your deposition weren't you asked this question, and didn't you give this answer:

Q: Now Officer Bier, how was Watkins walking when he was inside the store?
A: I can't say for sure. My view into the store was obstructed.

A: Yes, that is what it says.

You want to confine your questions to what the witness said at the deposition, not what the witness remembers now. Your opponent will no doubt do redirect examination to try to rehabilitate the witness.

Impeachment by Inconsistent Oral Deposition - **Short Form**

On direct examination, the witness said, "The light was <u>green</u>."

You want to impeach with the witness' deposition that says,
"The light was <u>red</u>."

Q: On direct examination you said the light was green?
A: Yes.

Q: Even though on direct examination you said that the light was green, at the deposition weren't you asked the following question, and didn't you give the following answer?
Q: What color was the light?
A: The light was red.
A: Yes.

Impeachment by Inconsistent Oral Deposition - Long Form

On direct examination, the witness said, "The light was green."
You want to impeach with the witness' deposition that says,
"The light was red."

Highlight the inconsistency
Q. On direct examination you said the light was green. [A: Yes]
Q. There is no question in your mind about that? [A: No question.]

Lock the witness into the testimony (you can omit this step)
Q. Have you ever said anything different? [No]
Q. Are you sure it was green? [Yes]
Q. Isn't it true that the light was in fact red? [No]

Build up the impeaching document
Q. You remember coming to my office to answer some questions?
Q. You came for a deposition on July 11, last year?
Q. I asked you questions, and you gave me answers, isn't that right?
Q. Your lawyer sat next to you while you answered?
Q. A court reporter took down your answers?
Q. That reporter gave you an oath to tell the truth?
Q. You agreed to tell the truth?
Q. After that deposition, the Q's and A's were typed up and you had a chance to read them over?
Q. After making sure it was correct, you signed it didn't you?
Q. This is your signature, isn't it?
Q. This deposition was just four months after the accident?
Q. Even though on direct examination you said that the light was green, at the deposition weren't you asked the following question, and didn't you give the following answer?
   Q: What color was the light?
   A: The light was red.

Impeachment by Inconsistent Oral Statement

(Assuming only the cross-examining lawyer heard the inconsistent statement)

Assume that although Bier testified on direct exam that "Watkins stumbled and almost fell inside the store," Bier was overheard outside the courtroom say to a person who is not available to testify, "I never really saw Watkins stumble inside the store." However, only the lawyer for Cut-Rate Liquor heard Bier's statement.

This is an inconsistent oral statement. Unlike most inconsistent statements, this one was not made prior to the in-court testimony on direct exam. This statement was made after the in-court testimony.

This fact pattern presents a special problem if the lawyer was the only person who overhead the statement. If Bier denies making the statement, the cross-examiner does not have a witness who could be called to the stand to complete the impeachment of Bier. So, if no one other that the lawyer overhead the statement, what can the lawyer do? Although no evidence rule prohibits the lawyer from testifying, rules of professional conduct in most jurisdictions would prohibit prevent the lawyer from testifying. What can the lawyer do?

Probably the best solution would be for the impeaching lawyer to be as detailed as possible during the cross leading up to the impeaching question. If the trier of fact believes the details, the trier of fact might believe that Bier also made the final statement ("I never saw him stumble inside the store.").

The detailed cross could do something like this.

Q: During the break, you went outside the courtroom, right?

Q: And you sat on the bench outside?

Q: You sat next to a man wearing a blue shirt, right?

Q: And the two of you had a conversation?

Q: You talked for about 5 minutes, right?

Q: "Even though you said on direct exam in court just 30 minutes ago that Watkins stumbled and almost fell in the store when he was at the counter, didn't you say to a man on a bench outside this courtroom just 10 minutes ago, "I never really saw Watkins stumble inside the store?"

Using Learned Treatises

FRE 803. Exceptions to the Rule Against Hearsay — Regardless of Whether the Declarant Is Available as a Witness
The following are not excluded by the rule against hearsay, regardless of whether the declarant is available as a witness:
(18) Statements in Learned Treatises, Periodicals, or Pamphlets.
A statement contained in a treatise, periodical, or pamphlet if:
   (A) the statement is <u>called to the attention of an expert</u> witness on cross-examination or relied on by the expert on direct examination; and
   (B) the publication is established as a <u>reliable authority</u> by the expert's admission or testimony, by another expert's testimony, or by judicial notice.
If admitted, the statement may be <u>read</u> into evidence <u>but not received</u> as an exhibit.

Perspective: 38 states have a similar or identical rule;
7 state rules only allow use of the treatise for impeachment (California, Florida, Georgia, Michigan, Oregon, Tennessee, and Virginia); 5 states have no rule (Illinois, Massachusetts, Missouri, New York, and Pennsylvania).

---

3 Key Points for Using the Learned Treatise

To use a learned treatise on either direct or cross-examination, under FRE 803(18)
1) there must be an expert <u>on the witness stand,</u>
2) the treatise has been established as a <u>reliable authority</u>, and
3) the statement may be <u>only read</u> into the record, but the treatise cannot be physically introduced into evidence.

Learned Treatises:
Use on Direct Exam to Support Your Expert
R803(18) – Hearsay Exception

After an expert testifies that it is not possible to determine if the plaintiff's epileptic seizures are caused by the plaintiff's auto accident, the following questioning takes place to use a learned treatise to support the expert's opinion. This is an example of using a "paper expert," or said another way, getting the opinion of two experts but only calling one as a witness.

Q: Dr. Rosenberg, are you familiar with the text called Medicine written by Dr. Mark Fishman?
A: Yes

Q: Let me show you proposed exhibit #1. What is it?
A: It is the book called Medicine written by Dr. Mark Fishman.

Q: Is it a recognized as a reliable authority in the field of medicine?
A: Yes

Q: What does the Fishman text say about the causes of epileptic seizures?
A: On page 135, Fishman says that a cause is found for seizures in less than 25% of the cases.

Using a learned treatise as a hearsay exception can only done by reading the treatise to the trier of fact, but not by physically introducing the treatise into evidence. FRE 803(18)

Learned Treatises:
Use on Cross to Attack
the Opposing Expert
FRE 803(18) – Hearsay Exception

After establishing that Mark Fishman's text called "Medicine" is a reliable authority in the field of medicine, either by your expert, or by your opponent's expert, or by judicial notice (Note: judges seldom take such judicial notice), the lawyer below uses the learned treatise on cross examination to contradict the opposing party's expert witness. A statement in a treatise can be used to impeach the opponent's expert and as substantive evidence (meaning for the truth of the statement – this is a hearsay exception).

Q: Dr. Barron, you testified during your direct examination that Mr. Fulbright's epilepsy was caused by the auto accident, right?
A: Yes.

Q: Dr., there is no medical evidence that Mr. Fulbright showed any clinical evidence of brain injury immediately after the incident is there?
A: That's correct.

Q: And no evidence of a skull fracture?
A: That's also correct.

Q: And no evidence of bloody spinal fluid, right?
A: Correct again.

Q: Dr., doesn't the text called, Medicine, written by Mark Fishman, indicate on page 132 that the four symptoms most commonly found with epileptic seizures are 1) loss of consciousness, 2) clinical evidence of brain injury immediately after the incident, 3) skull fracture, and 4) bloody spinal fluid?
A: Yeah, Fishman does say that.

Q: Your Honor, no further questions.

Voicemail, Phone Conversations, Recorded Phone Conversations

There is nothing special about the identification of a telephone call. Authentication for voice identification is covered in FRE 901(b)(5)&(6).

Do you know X?

How do you know X?

How long have you known X?

Have you ever spoken with X on the phone?

How often have you spoken with X on the phone?

On [the day in question] did you have a phone conversation with X?

Who initiated that call?

[If **your** witness initiated the call]

> How did you make the call? [Ans: used contacts list on my cell phone; used recent call list on cell phone; used landline]
>
> Was their name already in your cell phone from previous calls to them?
>
> Did you recognize the voice when your call was answered?
>
> Who were you talking to?

(Continued on next page)

[If the **other party** initiated the call]

Could you tell who was calling you?

How could you tell who was calling you? [Name appeared on my cell phone]

Why did their name appear in your cell phone? [I had name in my contacts list from many previous calls]

Who was on the phone when you answered the call? [The defendant]

How did you know that? [We have talked many times before. I recognized his voice.]

What did he say during that call?

Digital Evidence
Electronically Stored Information – ESI

Electronically Stored Information (EIS) includes emails, text messages, websites, fax, social media, computer printouts, and other digital records. Although evidence professors will tell you that the classic rules of evidence, created long before cell phones, computers, and the Internet, are more than adequate for the new digital world, some people may doubt it.

Yet truly, introducing digital evidence in court still does apply the same basic "HARROWing" principles found in all evidence codes – whether introducing physical items or digital evidence.

"HARROWing" is my mnemonic to remind us of evidence principles to consider when introducing physical pieces of evidence, especially physical evidence with words on or in it. HARROWing - defined as extremely distressing, agonizing, excruciating, torturing, painful, and causing physical or psychological pain – is how many new lawyers describe their experience trying to introduce evidence

H = Hearsay; FRE 800s
A= Authentication; FRE 900s
R= FRE R401 relevancy (sometime called "logical relevancy);
R= FRE403 (sometimes called "legal Relevancy);
OW = FRE 1000s Original Writings (traditionally known as Best Evidence).

The same rules of evidence apply to ESI as they do to paper and physical evidence. The most challenging foundational issues for digital evidence are establishing:1) who created the digital evidence (the author), and 2) has it been altered?

A Variety of Standards

Different standards have developed in various jurisdictions for authenticating digital evidence.

The Texas courts, and probably most jurisdictions, use an authentication standard identical to the standard used for traditional forms of evidence – "evidence sufficient to support a finding (R 901). The Texas standard can be thought of and remembered by the state's placement on a map – it is a lower standard.

However, the <u>Maryland courts, and a few others</u>, have developed a higher standard – like Maryland's placement on a map. Maryland courts seem to require that the proponent of digital evidence prove that the digital evidence has not been altered or hacked, it comes from a certain source, and that <u>no one other than the owner could have used the electronic device to send or post the message</u>. This view of EIS authentication is concerned about "voodoo information taken from the Internet." It creates a standard that can seldom be met. However, in more recent cases Maryland courts have backed away from that high standard and seem now to favor a more traditional approach for authenticating digital evidence.

The Grimm, Joseph & Capra article, Best Practices for Authenticating Digital Evidence 69 Baylor L.Rev. 1 (2017) is a great source for understanding factors in authenticating digital evidence. That article presents an overview of how FRE 104(a) and 104(b) interact in the authentication process and the article argues that digital evidence should be authenticated requiring only evidence

"<u>sufficient to support a finding,</u>" - which is a low standard.

The authors offer the opinion that,

> "<u>Generally speaking, it will be a rare case in which an item of digital evidence cannot be authenticated.</u>"

The article covers various ways to authenticate digital evidence. Most helpful will be the examples of various types of circumstantial evidence that would qualify as "distinctive characteristics" under FRE 901(b)(4). Additional, less frequently used methods of authenticating evidence are also covered, such as, personal knowledge of a witness, business records (in some email situations), jury comparison, and production in discovery.

Distinctive Characteristics and Circumstantial Evidence Used to Authenticate Emails and Text Messages as Having Been Sent by A Particular Person
Or
As Having Been Received by A Particular Person

There are many possible ways to use circumstantial evidence to qualify as "distinctive characteristics" to authenticate Electronically Stored Information (ESI) under FRE 901(b)(4) Distinctive Characteristics and the Like. Appearance, contents, substance, internal patterns, or other distinctive characteristics of the item taken together with all the circumstances are almost endless.

The Grimm, Joseph & Capra article offers many extremely valuable suggestions about circumstantial evidence which can be considered "distinctive characteristics" and used to authenticate digital evidence under R901(b)(4).

For example, when laying the foundation for an email or text, consider:
1) information in or about the email or text
2) information outside the email or text itself that leads back to the author
3) forensic information, and
4) information outside the email or text itself indicating receipt of the message.

Factors suggested by Grimm, Joseph, and Capra used to authenticate authorship or receipt of a message include:

1) information in or about the email or text, such as:
- the email address, email signature, a nickname, a screen name, initials, a moniker, the author's customary use of emoji or emoticons, a writing style (including phrases and abbreviations frequently used by the author), referring to facts only the author or small group of people would know about, facts uniquely tied to the author, information about the author's family, photos of the author, items of importance to the author such as a car or a pet, and other such information

2) information outside the email or text itself that leads back to the author, such as:

- the email was part of a chain or series of emails from the same person, the claimed author told the witness to expect an email from the author, the author orally repeats its content soon after the email is sent, the author discusses the contents of the email with the third party, the author leaves a voicemail substantially of the same content, and other such information

3) forensic information, such as:

- an email's hash values or testimony from a forensic witness that the email came from a particular device at a particular time, and other such information

4) information outside the email or text itself indicating receipt of the message, such as:

- a reply was received by the sender that came from the recipient, later conduct of the recipient reflects knowledge of the contents of the sent message, later communication of the recipient reflects knowledge of the message, and the message was received and accessed on an electronic device in the possession of the recipient, and other such information.

Presenting the Digital Evidence from a Cell Phone in Court

- Print the page from the phone and use the printout in court.
- If a photo comes from a cell phone, attach the picture to an email, and then print the picture from a computer.
- Screenshot the information (picture, text message, email, social media post), email it, then print from a computer.

Self-Authentication for Digital Evidence

Recent amendments to the Federal Rules of Evidence allow for self-authentication of certified records

– See FRE 902(11)(13)(14)

Digital Evidence and Self-Authentication

FRE 902 Self-authentication
(11) Certified Domestic Records of a Regularly Conducted Activity. The original or a copy of a domestic record that meets the requirements of Rule 803(6)(A)-(C), as shown by a certification of the custodian or another qualified person that complies with a federal statute or a rule prescribed by the Supreme Court. Before the trial or hearing, the proponent must give an adverse party reasonable written notice of the intent to offer the record — and must make the record and certification available for inspection — so that the party has a fair opportunity to challenge them.

> 39 states have similar or identical rules. Many states have created forms for self-authentication of business records.

FRE 902(13) (Added to FRE Dec. 2017)
(13) Certified Records Generated by an Electronic Process or System. A record generated by an electronic process or system that produces an accurate result, as shown by a certification of a qualified person that complies with the certification requirements of Rule 902(11) or (12). The proponent must also meet the notice requirements of Rule 902(11).
[This rule covers text messages, cell phone photos,
GPS data, and other ESI]

> The following 10 states have this rule:
> Alabama, Arizona, Illinois, Maryland, Mississippi,
> North Dakota, Ohio, Pennsylvania, Utah, and Wyoming

FRE 902(14) Certified Data Copied from an Electronic Device, Storage Medium, or File. Data copied from an electronic device, storage medium, or file, if authenticated by a process of digital identification, as shown by a certification of a qualified person that complies with the certification requirements of Rule 902(11) or (12). The proponent also must meet the notice requirements of Rule 902(11).

> The following 10 states have this rule:
> Alabama, Arizona, Illinois, Maryland, Mississippi,
> North Dakota, Ohio, Pennsylvania, Utah, and Wyoming

Email – Witness is the Sender (Outgoing Email)

Q: How did you notify Cut-Rate about …
A: I sent an email to Dan Jones

Q: What email address did you use?
A: DJones@Cutrate.com

Q: How do you know that was the correct address?
A: He and I have email back and forth for a few months, and all of his emails to me came from that email address

Q: Let me show you what has been marked as plaintiff's proposed exhibit #1.

Q: What is it? (A printout of the email I sent to Jones that day.).

Q: How do you know that? (I wrote it. I remember it. It was in my "sent mail" folder.)

Q: Your Honor I offer the exhibit into evidence.

Email – Witness is the Recipient (Incoming Email)

Do you know Dan Jones?

How do you know him?

Are you familiar with the email address DJones@Cutrate.com?

Have you received emails from Dan Jones in the past?

Have you sent emails to Dan Jones at that address?

Has he responded to your emails from that email address?

Is that email address in your email contacts?

In late April, did you receive an email from Dan Jones about selling liquor?

Did you recognize email address as being from Dan Jones?

I am handing you what has been marked as proposed exhibit #7. Do you recognize it?

What is it? (A: The email from Dan Jones)

Why would you say that's an email from Dan Jones?
[provide information about distinctive characteristics of this email]

How did you get a paper copy of this email? (A: I printed it out.)

Is this a true and accurate printout of that email?

Your Honor, I offer the proposed exhibit into evidence.

> [The email reads: "I might be getting fired. They caught me selling booze to drunks again."]

Text Message

Received by Witness

Do you know Y?

Do you communicate with Y on a regular basis?

In what ways to you communicate with Y?

Did you receive a text message from the Y [recently; on or about _ date, on the topic of ..., etc.]?

Would you recognize a printout of the message if you were to see it again?

Let me show you what has been marked as proposed exhibit # 1. Do you recognize it?

What is it? [Ans: A screenshot from my cell phone]

How do you know that this is a message from Y? [It is similar to other messages I have received from Y in that ...]

How did it appear when it arrived on your phone? [Showed up under the name and with the picture I had previously assigned to Y]

What other distinctive characteristics did you notice about the message? [provide as many as distinctive characteristics possible]

Is it a fair and accurate representation of the text message you received [recently; on or about _ date, on the topic of visiting your son, etc.]?

Has it been altered in any way?

I would like to enter the proposed exhibit into evidence

Social Media
Facebook, Instagram, Snapchat, Twitter, and other Posts

Do you know B?

How long have you known him?

Are you familiar with Facebook?

Does B have a Facebook account?

Have you seen posts by B on his Facebook account in the past?

How do you know that B made those posts? [provide distinctive characteristics]

Have you seen a posting on B's Facebook account about [the matter in question]?

Let the record reflect that I am handing you what has been marked as proposed exhibit 12 and ask if you can identify it?

What is it?

Is that a screenshot of the Facebook posting by B about ___?

What day did you take the screenshot?

Is it a true and accurate screenshot of that posting?

Is the post still on B's account? [Ask this question only if it is currently on the account.]

I offer the proposed exhibit into evidence.

Internet Website – Web Posting

Did you visit Professor John Barkai's webpage? [Yes]

How did you access it? [Googled "John Barkai" on my phone]

How did you find his page?
    Ans: "Yes, I clicked on the link that said
        "Prof. John Barkai Homepage.""

What did you find when you clicked on that link for the homepage?
    Ans: I found his list of courses and other posts.

Did you click on any particular link?
    Ans: I clicked Hawaii Rules of Evidence (HRE) Book Page

What did you find on that page when you clicked on it?
    A: I found a link to buy from Amazon a copy of several
    different evidence handbooks.

Let me show you what's been marked as proposed exhibit # 14. Can
    you identify it?
    A: Yes. It's a screenshot of that webpage with instructions
    about how to buy books from Amazon.

Was that screenshot a print of the page from his website?
    A: Yes, I printed it myself.

Is this exhibit a fair and accurate copy of that webpage?　[Yes]

Has this exhibit of the screenshot been altered or otherwise change
from the image on your phone in any way?　　[No]

I offer the exhibit into evidence.

Fax – Incoming

Does your office have a fax machine?

Do you send outgoing faxes?

Do you receive incoming faxes?

Have you received purchase orders from the defendant by fax in the past?

Let me show you plaintiff's proposed exhibit # 27 and ask if you can identify it? [A: Yes. I can]

What is it? [A: A fax I received about six months ago from the defendant]

Why do you say this fax came from the defendant?
A: There are number of factors in addition to the document being written on the defendant's letterhead stationery. The fax is signed by the head of defendant's purchasing department, and I am familiar with her signature from our past dealings. Further, imprinted on the bottom of this fax sheet is the fax number for the defendant's company, and I have faxed prior documents to the defendant by using that number. Finally, the document relates to the purchase of some equipment that I had discussed with the defendant's head of purchasing just a few hours before the fax arrived at my office.

Is this document in the same or substantially the same condition as it was when you received it?   [A: Yes, it is exactly the same.]

There have been no alterations or changes? [A: None whatsoever.]

Your Honor, I move that this proposed exhibit be admitted into evidence.

Expert Opinions

Washington follows the Frye "general acceptance" test.
See, State V. Riker, 869 P.2d 43 (Wash. 1994).

Admissibility of Expert Testimony.
The majority of states have explicitly adopted the Daubert (FRE702) standard.
A minority of states use either the Frye ("general acceptance") standard or some combination of Daubert and Frye standards.
Additionally, "general acceptance" is part of the Daubert standard.

Four Part Expert Opinion Foundation and Testimony

1. Elicit the background and qualifications of the expert
2. Tender or offer the witness as expert in a particular field (e.g., 'general medicine.")
   – Opponent is allowed to voir dire (test qualifications by cross examination limited to the expert's qualifications, but not the facts of this case)
3. Offer the expert's opinion or conclusion (to a particular standard such as "reasonable medical certainty") FRE 702
4. Offer the basis for opinion FRE703
   – Including reasonable reliance on inadmissible evidence
   – Disclosure of inadmissible evidence?

Three Simple Questions

1) Q: "Do you have an opinion as to whether…
2) Q: "What is that opinion?"
3) Q: "How did you reach that opinion?
   A: [including inadmissible information reasonably relied upon by experts in the particular field, FRE 703]

How to Start

The expert witness examination normally starts with questions to establish the witness' qualifications to testify as an expert.

Topics for Background and Qualifications of an Expert:

- formal education, work experience, number of previous times retained, qualified, and testified as an expert, in which courts, on-the-job training, non-degree training courses, publications in the field, teaching in the field, memberships in related professional associations, and any other topics relevant to showing the person is an expert.

Tender / Offer

After presenting the expert's background and qualifications, in jurisdictions where the judge must "certify" or "find" that the witness is an expert and is to permitted to testify as an expert, the lawyer presenting the expert then "tenders" or "offers" the witness to the judge as an expert, stating the field of expertise.

"I offer/tender Mr. X as an expert in the field of…"

"I ask the court to certify Ms. Y as an expert in the field of …"

Can you call the expert an "expert?"

After any voir dire (a limited cross examination to test the qualifications of the witness) by opposing counsel and objections, the judge rules on whether the expert can continue to testify as an expert. Some courts do not allow the lawyer to use the word "expert" to refer to the expert witness. but the judge is still changed with the responsibility of determining if the witness is qualified as an expert. Yet no one uses the word "expert" in front of lay fact finders. The apparent reason for such a practice is, as explained below.

The 2000 Advisory Committee Notes to the amendment to Federal Rule of Evidence 702 says, in part:

> "…The use of the term "expert" in the Rule does not, however, mean that a jury should actually be informed that a qualified witness is testifying as an "expert." Indeed, there is much to be said for a practice that prohibits the use of the term "expert" by both the parties and the court at trial. Such a practice "ensures that trial courts do not inadvertently put their stamp of authority" on a witness's opinion, and protects against the jury's being "overwhelmed by the so-called 'experts'."

More Tenders/Offers of the expert

"We believe that Mr. Taylor should be permitted to offer his opinions in this case."

"I tender Dr. Barron as an expert in the field of family medicine and request that she be allowed to testify as such.

"I offer Dr. Rosenberg as an expert in the field of neurology."

"Judge, we ask that the court accept Dr. Shigeta as an expert in civil engineering."

Offering the Opinion

Traditionally, the opinion is delivered in a two-question sequence:

    Q1: Do you have an opinion as ....?

    A: Yes

    Q2: What is that opinion?

"Do you have an opinion, <u>within a reasonable degree of scientific certainty</u>, as to the time of death of Ms. X?"

"Do you have an opinion, <u>to a reasonable degree of medical probability</u>, as to whether the motorcycle accident caused Mr. Fulbright's epilepsy?"

"Do you have an opinion, <u>to a reasonable degree of engineering certainty</u>, as to whether the XXX caused the bridge to fail?"

"Do you have an opinion whether Mr. X suffered a brain damage as a result of the fight?"

Standards for Stating an Expert's Opinion

There are no minimum standards under FRE 702 describing how "good" an expert's opinion must be to be stated in court. By case law, some courts and jurisdictions require that the standard must be stated to a

    "reasonable degree of [medical] <u>certainty</u>," or a

    "reasonable degree of [scientific] <u>probability.</u>"

Other jurisdictions simply allow an expert to state an opinion without any specific qualification.

    "What did your examination reveal?"

The above standards of "certainty" and "probability" are vague and rather unhelpful standards to a lay jury or courts-martial member who might be able to understand percentages, but who are given no guidance to the certainty or probability. Do those standards mean 51%, 65%, 75%, 85%, 95%, etc.? "Preponderance of the evidence" does have an associated percentage (50%+), but terms such as "sufficient to support a finding," "clear and convincing," "beyond a reasonable doubt," as well as "certainty" and "probability" do not. Simply, use whatever standard your judge and jurisdiction require. In an attempt to be persuasive, some lawyers ask the experts questions like:

"How positive are you of your opinion?"
"What is the degree of your certainty?"

Inadmissible Information Reasonably Relied Upon

Experts can base their opinions on hearsay and other inadmissible evidence. FRE 703 says in part:

> "If experts in the particular field would reasonably rely on those kinds of facts or data in forming an opinion on the subject, they need not be admissible for the opinion to be admitted."

You should have in your tool chest of questions this question. "Is that the type of information reasonably relied upon by experts in your field?"

Remember

Whoever has the Biggest, Most Qualified Expert Might Win

Because opposing parties usually present opposing experts who have reached opposing conclusions, the advocacy principle is for you to try to present a more qualified and more credible expert than your opponent's expert. If "your" expert's testimony and conclusions are believed on the issue in dispute, you are more likely to win your case.

Books by John Barkai

Federal Rules of Evidence Handbook with Common Objections & Evidentiary Foundations

Humor in Negotiations & ADR: Cartoon Caption Contest Winners from the ABA Dispute Resolution Magazine

Humor in Trial Evidence: Cartoon Caption Contest Winners and Challenges from My Evidence Class

Military Rules of Evidence Handbook with Common Objections & Evidentiary Foundations

Negotiation and Mediation Communication Gambits for Breaking Impasses and More: What Do I Say When I Want To ...

The Pocket Guide to Common Trial Objections & Evidentiary Foundations

The following evidence books (for all 50 states and many other jurisdictions) in my Handbooks with Common Objections & Evidentiary Foundations series are available exclusively on Amazon for the following states:

Alabama	Idaho	Missouri	Pennsylvania **
Alaska	Illinois	Montana	Rhode Island
Arizona	Indiana	Nebraska	South Carolina
Arkansas	Iowa	Nevada	South Dakota
California **	Kansas	New Hampshire	Tennessee
Colorado	Kentucky	New Jersey	Texas **
Connecticut	Louisiana	New Mexico	Utah
Delaware	Maine **	New York	Vermont
District of Columbia	Maryland	North Carolina	Virginia
Florida **	Massachusetts	North Dakota	Washington
Georgia	Michigan **	Ohio	West Virginia
Hawaii **	Minnesota	Oklahoma	Wisconsin
	Mississippi	Oregon	Wyoming

Pacific Island countries and other U.S. affiliated jurisdictions	
American Samoa	Northern Mariana Islands
Chuuk	Pohnpei
Federated States of Micronesia	Puerto Rico
Guam	Republic of Palau
Kosrae	U.S. Virgin Islands
Marshall Islands	Yap

** I also published "Just the Rules" books for these seven states.

Massachusetts, Missouri, and New York do not have formal rules of evidence, but Massachusetts and New York do publish state "Guides" to evidence

To find John Barkai's evidence and cartoon books

1. Go to the Amazon website – www.Amazon.com

2. Enter into the search bar: - John Barkai

3. For a particular state, enter into the Amazon search bar
- John Barkai [state name]

History and Restyling of the Federal Rules of Evidence

The Federal Rules of Evidence (FRE) were adopted in 1975. Approximately 46 states have adopted evidence codes, by statute or court rule, which are patterned on the FRE. The states without FRE based evidence codes are California, Kansas, Missouri, and New York. The California Evidence Code took effect in 1965 and is quite different in structure than any other state evidence code.

Although most states modeled their evidence rules after the FRE, almost every state has some evidence provisions which are different from the federal rules and some states have very significant differences.

The FRE were "restyled" in 2011 to
> "make them more easily understood and to make style and terminology consistent throughout the rules. These changes are intended to be stylistic only. There is no intent to change any result in any ruling on evidence admissibility.... The [Restyling] Committee made special efforts to reject any purposed style improvement that might result in a substantive change in the application of a rule." --- See Restyled Rules Committee Note for Restyled Rules of Evidence.

So far, at least thirteen (13) states, have restyled their rules of evidence: Arizona (2012), Delaware (2017), Idaho (2018), Indiana (2013), Iowa (2017), Maine (2015), Mississippi (2016), New Hampshire (2017), Pennsylvania (2013), South Dakota (2016), Texas (2014), Utah (2012), and West Virginia (2014). The Military (2013) and the Commonwealth of the Northern Mariana Islands (2015) have also restyled.

An excellent resource for understanding the differences between the FRE and the evidence rules of other states is the multi-volume treatise, Wharton's Criminal Evidence by Bergman and Hollander. This treatise is available in many law libraries and is available on Westlaw, where it is called CRIMEVID database. Despite included the word "Criminal" in its title, the treatise discusses evidence issues (criminal and civil) but does not cover FRE 407, 408, and 411, and it does not cover the criminal topic of confrontation.

Washington's Certified Business Records
See Revised Code of Washington (RCW)

RCW 5.45.020 Business records as evidence.

A record of an act, condition or event, shall in so far as relevant, be competent evidence if the custodian or other qualified witness testifies to its identity and the mode of its preparation, and if it was made in the regular course of business, at or near the time of the act, condition or event, and if, in the opinion of the court, the sources of information, method and time of preparation were such as to justify its admission.

RCW 10.96.030 Authenticity of records—Verification—Affidavit, declaration, or certification.

(1) Upon written request from the applicant, or if ordered by the court, the recipient of criminal process shall verify the authenticity of records that it produces by providing an affidavit, declaration, or certification that complies with subsection (2) of this section. The requirements of RCW 5.45.020 regarding business records as evidence may be satisfied by an affidavit, declaration, or certification that complies with subsection (2) of this section, without the need for testimony from the custodian of records, regardless of whether the business records were produced by a foreign or Washington state entity.

(2) To be admissible without testimony from the custodian of records, business records must be accompanied by an affidavit, declaration, or certification by its record custodian or other qualified person that includes contact information for the witness completing the document and attests to the following:

(a) The witness is the custodian of the record or sets forth evidence that the witness is qualified to testify about the record;

(b) The record was made at or near the time of the act, condition, or event set forth in the record by, or from information transmitted by, a person with knowledge of those matters;

(c) The record was made in the regular course of business;

(d) The identity of the record and the mode of its preparation; and

(e) Either that the record is the original or that it is a duplicate that accurately reproduces the original.

(3) A party intending to offer a record into evidence under this section must provide written notice of that intention to all adverse parties, and must make the record and affidavit, declaration, or certification available for inspection sufficiently in advance of their offer into evidence to provide an adverse party with a fair opportunity to challenge them. A motion opposing admission in evidence of the record shall be made and determined by the court before trial and with sufficient time to allow the party offering the record time, if the motion is granted, to produce the custodian of the record or other qualified person at trial, without creating hardship on the party or on the custodian or other qualified person.

(4) Failure by a party to timely file a motion under subsection (4) of this section shall constitute a waiver of objection to admission of the evidence, but the court for good cause shown may grant relief from the waiver. When the court grants relief from the waiver, and thereafter determines the custodian of the record shall appear, a continuance of the trial may be granted to provide the proponent of the record sufficient time to arrange for the necessary witness to appear.

(5) Nothing in this section precludes either party from calling the custodian of record of the record or other witness to testify regarding the record.

Dedication

To my wife Linda and my adult twin daughters Hope and Leah,
who bring me so much joy and enrich my life
and
to the hundreds of my former evidence and clinical students
who learned these rules of evidence with me
over the past 50 years
at the William S. Richardson School of Law
at the University of Hawaii
and
Wayne State Law School in Detroit.

About the Authors

Professor Barkai is a former Detroit Michigan criminal trial lawyer, a fulltime law professor for 50 years, and a Professor of Law at the William S. Richardson School of Law at the University of Hawaii for 45 years. He has taught evidence since 1981 and has been the Director, and now Co-Director, of the Law School's Clinical Program since 1978. He has been a member of the Hawaii Supreme Court's Standing Committee on the Rules of Evidence since 1993. He has a B.B.A, M.B.A, and J.D, all from the University of Michigan. For the past 50 years, he has taught a criminal clinic in which his students try traffic and minor criminal cases under the state student practice rule. He has published evidence handbooks similar to this one for all 50 states as well as 15 other jurisdictions from American Samoa to the U.S. Virgin Islands. He also has evidence and negotiation & ADR cartoon books on Amazon as well as a book on effective communication for negotiation and mediation.

Kira J. Goo, J.D., is a 2021 graduate of the William S. Richardson School of Law, University of Hawai'i at Manoa, a member of the Hawaii Bar, and an associate at Leong Kunihiro Brooke & Kim. She has a B.A. from Seattle University, worked at the State Public Defender's Office before law school. She was the executive editor for the Asia-Pacific Law & Policy Journal. She externed for Associate Justice Sabrina S. McKenna of the Hawai'i Supreme Court and State Circuit Court Judge Bert. I Ayabe. She also was a research assistant for Professor Barkai.